Treasures
of
Northeast Ohio

The first complete reference to museums, historic villages, and historic districts plus one cemetery in Ohio's northeast quadrant; includes the Columbus, Zanesville, and Cambridge areas.

by Joseph C. Quinlan

Published by Global Editorial Co., P.O. Box 210058, Cleveland, Ohio 44121

Treasures of Northeast Ohio

Library of Congress Catalog Card Number: 00 130093

ISBN Number: 0-9678003-0-7

Published by Global Editorial Co., Cleveland, Ohio

Manufactured in the United States of America

Preface

My wife Marjorie and I have been retired for several years. One of the activities we enjoy doing together is taking short trips. Lasting anywhere from two hours to eight, these excursions take us to factory outlet malls, zoos, Amishland bric-a-brac stores, and even mills and factories.

Destinations such as these are fine, but our favorite type of excursion involves going to a museum or historic village, plus an enticing restaurant nearby. Thanks mainly to magazine listings, it has been easy to find the restaurants, but locating and evaluating museums and villages has been more difficult.

True, a number of periodicals contain brief listings of these facilities, but without exception, the listings don't contain enough information. Worse yet, they don't give you a reason to spend the time, money, and effort to visit any given facility.

Tthere's a distinct need for the book you're reading. After more than three years of stumbling along without adequate resources, I finally realized the nature of the need, and decided I should fill it myself. Hence this book.

Before I forget, this is a good place to thank all the museum staffers who generously provided information, checked my writeups for accuracy, and offered many tips and words of encouragement. Without their help, this book couldn't exist.

Joseph C. Quinlan
October, 1999
Cleveland, Ohio

Table of Contents

Introduction, p. 18

Museum Listings, pp. 21–172

This table lists cities and towns alphabetically; museums, historic villages, historic districts, etc., are listed alphabetically under the name of each city or town.

SECTION 1 –– AKRON THROUGH CAMBRIDGE

SECTION 2 -- CANAL FULTON THROUGH CLEVELAND

SECTION 3 -- COLUMBIANA
THROUGH GNADENHUTTEN

Geneva
Shandy Hall Museum, p. 92

Geneva-on-the-Lake
Ashtabula County History Museum, p. 169

Gnadenhutten
Gnadenhutten Historical Park, p. 92

SECTION 4 -- GRANVILLE THROUGH MENTOR

Granville
Granville Historical Museum, p. 94
Granville Lifestyle Museum, p. 94
Robbins Hunter Museum, p. 95

Hiram
John Johnson Farm House, p. 96

Jefferson
J.R. Giddings Law Office Museum, p. 169
Jefferson Depot Railroad Museum, p. 97
Victorian Perambulator Museum, p. 98

Kent
Kent State Hearing Aid Museum, p. 169
Kent State University Museum, p. 99

Kenton
Dougherty House, p. 169
Hardin County Historical Museums, p. 169

Kidron
Kidron Community Hist. Soc. Museum, p. 99

Killbuck
Killbuck Valley Museum, p. 169

Kirtland
Euclid Beach Amusement Park Museum, p. 170
Kirtland Temple Historic Center, p. 100
N.K. Whitney Store Museum, p. 101

Lakeside
Heritage Hall Museum, p. 101

Lakewood
Oldest Stone House Museum, p. 102

Lenox
Lenox Rural Museum, p. 170

Lexington
Richland County Museum, p. 103

Lisbon
Fort Tuscaroras Museum, p. 170
Lisbon Historic District, p. 103

Lorain
Moore House Museum, p. 104

Loudonville
Cleo Redd Fisher Museum, p. 105
(Also called Mohican Hist. Soc. Museum)

Lucas
Malabar Farm, p. 106

Mansfield
Kingwood Center, p. 107
Living Bible Museum, p. 170
Oak Hill Cottage, p. 107
Ohio State Reformatory, p. 108

Maple Heights
Little Red Schoolhouse Museum, p. 109

SECTION 5 -- MILAN THROUGH ORRVILLE

14

15

Wellington
Spirit of '76 Museum, p. 154

SECTION 7 -- WESTERVILLE THROUGH ZOAR

Westerville
Hanby House, p. 155
Ross C. Purdy Museum of Ceramics, p. 155

Westlake
Clague House Museum, p. 156

Willard
B&O Railroad Museum, p. 157

Willoughby
History Center of Willoughby, p. 171

Willowick
U.S. Aviation Museum, p. 158

Windsor
Christ Episcopal Church Museum, p. 172

Wooster
College of Wooster Art Museum, p. 159
Wayne County Hist. Soc. Campus, p. 159

Worthington
Worthington Museums, p. 160

Youngstown
Arms Family Museum, p. 161
Butler Institute of American Art, p. 162
McDonough Museum of Art, p. 172
Youngstown Historical Center, p. 162

Zanesville
Historic District of Zanesville, p. 163
Zanesville Art Center, p. 172

Zoar
Zoar Village State Memorial, p. 164

APPENDICES

Introduction

This guidebook should prove interesting and useful not only to retirees, but also to vacationers, business travelers with time to fill, and students of all ages who want to learn more about history, art, nature, autos, aerospace, general science, clothing fashions, or you name it. Some 26 major categories of interest are covered in the museums, villages, and historic districts listed in this book.

Visiting museums becomes a wonderful pastime. Besides offering countless discoveries, this activity can take place enjoyably in cold, wet, hot, humid, or windy weather, when outdoor activities are unpleasant if not impossible. You can visit and enjoy museums at any time of the year, in any weather.

Of all the facilities listed, about 27 percent are open from 5 to 7 months of the year, and 15 percent are open 8 to 11 months. The remaining 58 percent are open year around. No matter what the season or month, you'll find museums to visit.

This pastime is relatively inexpensive. Admission fees are low, and in most cases there's free parking next to the building or nearby. (I don't want to criticize other types of destinations, but compare museum prices with those of, say, amusement parks.)

I hope you find this book useful and interesting. If in perusing it you discover that a favorite museum has been left out, please notify the publisher in writing. We'll try to correct the omission in the next edition.

The same goes for omissions of useful information. If we didn't include some kind of data you think important and useful to many readers, let the publisher know in writing.

A few points of interest:

* The region covered, described as "Northeast Ohio," is bounded by a north-south line from Sandusky down to and including the Columbus area; and an east-west line from just south of Columbus due east to the Ohio River. This second line runs south of Interstate Highway I-70 to Moundsville, W.Va.

18

* To ensure a successful, enjoyable trip, you may find it best to call ahead and verify days and times the facility is open. This is important, because when a museum's hours are changed, the news usually doesn't go out very far or fast.

* The listings in this book refer to "free" and "for-pay" parking. The latter refers to metered parking on the street, or for-pay parking in a lot or parking deck. In some cases where parking facilities issue a ticket, the museum will stamp the ticket so you don't have to pay the parking fee. Check at the museum's front desk.

* If air-conditioning and/or wheelchair accessibility are important to you, call and ask about them. Also, bear in mind that most small historical museums -- a large percentage of museums listed in this book -- are old houses with stairs to climb. Few have air-conditioning.

* Visit historic villages, districts, and "campuses" on dry, warm days, not when it's raining, snowing, or quite hot or cold. A visit to these facilities calls for walking between buildings, often on dirt or grassy paths.

* Be sure to see the appendices at the end of this book. They offer alphabetical indexes of facilities by subject of interest and by name of facility.

* Before setting out to visit one facility, check to see if you and your companions may also like to visit one or more other facilities in the same town or area. For example, Sandusky is home to the Merry-Go-Round Museum, but Sandusky also has the Eleutheros Cooke House, Follett House Museum, and Sandusky Area Maritime Museum. This guidebook lists attractions alphabetically by name of town or city, then by name of attraction under each town or city.

* If you plan to visit a large facility such as a historic village or campus, allow at least two hours, preferably three. There's no way you can do justice to a facility such as Roscoe Village at Coshocton, or the Hale Farm and Village near Bath, in just one hour.

* It may be obvious, but we'll point it out anyway: Use this book in conjunction with a detailed map that has an alphabetical index of towns and cities. Planning and re-viewing your routes will make the trip more fun and less stressful.

* If you want to take snapshots inside the facilities, make sure the staff allows it. Some museums allow photography by available light only, not with flash; see the listings in this book. Also, check your camera batteries, flash batteries, and film before starting out on your trip.

When shooting, remember that flash bounces off glass and plexiglas shields in front of displays, producing large flares and poor pictures. Also, be aware that museums are essentially indoor facilities with tungsten or fluorescent lighting. If you're shooting with an SLR or an older rangefinder camera, and using daylight film, take along 80B and FL-D filters. These will help prevent over-all yellow or green tints in your pictures.

If you have a small point-and-shoot camera, consider using ASA 800 film, and lock out the flash when shooting glass-covered displays.

Happy browsing!

Museum Listings

SECTION 1 -- AKRON THROUGH CAMBRIDGE

Akron:
Akron Art Museum

Located downtown, the Akron Art Museum showcases regional, national, and international art from 1850 to the
present, with special focus on contemporary art and photography. For instance, the Museum recently staged a large
exhibition of Andy Warhol's pop-icon paintings and photographs, and an exhibition of 256 pieces of fine blown-glass
objects by Chihuly.

The Myers Sculpture Courtyard serves as an outdoor gallery for permanent, large-scale sculptures, as well as space
for "Downtown at Dusk" concerts in summer.

The Museum is open year around, seven days a week,
from 11:00 AM to 5:00 PM. Closed on major U.S. holidays. Admission is free.

Photography is not permitted. There's parking next to the
building; free for members, $2.00 for non-members.

Address: 70 E. Market St., Akron, OH 44308. Phone:
330-376-9185.

Akron:
Akron Police Dept. Museum

One highlight of this museum is a photo of the first motor-
ized police patrol wagon in the U.S. Built by Selle Gear
Co., Akron, it was powered by electric batteries. The Akron
Police Dept. acquired it in 1899.

Also on display here are collections of confiscated hand-
guns and other weapons, a "Breathalyzer" machine, old
police motorcycles, historic photos, infrared identification
equipment, and many police-related documents.

Open Mon.-Fri., 8:00 AM to 3:30 PM, year around.
Closed on Sat., Sun., and major U.S. holidays. Guided tours
can be arranged.

Admission is free. Photography, including use of flash, is allowed. There's for-pay parking across the street in the Summit County Parking Deck, and metered parking on nearby streets.

Address: Stubbs Justice Center, 217 S. High St., Akron, OH 44308. Phone: 330-375-2390. Fax: 330-375-2412.

Akron:
Copley Road Historic Homes

Owned and operated by the Summit County Historical Society, two historic homes -- the Simon Perkins Mansion and John Brown House -- commemorate great figures of Akron's past. The two buildings are situated across the road from one another.

Built in 1837 by Simon Perkins, Jr., son of Akron's founder, the mansion was occupied by the Perkins family and their descendants for over 100 years. Now a museum, this building displays furnishings and room decor that reflect the family's lifestyles for over three generations.

The first floor represents the style of living from the 1830's to the late 1860's. The second-floor decor represents three decades of Akron's industrial growth, from 1870 to 1900.

Just across the road, the John Brown House was occupied by abolitionist John Brown from 1844 to 1846. Soon to win fame in Kansas and at Harper's Ferry, he lived here while tending a flock of Merino sheep owned by his neighbor Simon Perkins, Jr. Brown moved on, but the house has been linked to him for over 150 years.

The John Brown House has been newly renovated inside and outside. The first floor holds a permanent exhibit on John Brown and his relationship with Simon Perkins, Jr., and other temporary exhibit space. The second floor is used for collection storage.

Both historic homes are open Tues.-Sun. from Feb. 1 to Dec. 24. Closed all Jan., and on Mon. and major U.S. holidays. Hours are 1:00 PM to 4:00 PM.

Admission: Adults $5.00, seniors (over 60) and children $4.00. In groups of 10 or more, adults pay $4.00 each.

No photography permitted. There is free parking on the mansion grounds as well as across the street.

Address: 550 Copley Rd., Akron, OH 44320. Phone: 330-535-1120. Fax: 330-376-6868.

Akron:
Inventure Place

Plenty of hands-on fun with gadgets, plus lively stories of inventions and inventors, await you at Inventure Place in downtown Akron. Opened in July, 1995, this 77,000-sq.-ft. facility with five floors has two main areas: the 23,000-sq.-ft. Inventors Workshop, and the multi-level National Inventors Hall of Fame.

The Workshop contains many interactive exhibits designed to interest adults as well as children. Here you can create a percussion band using laser beams, animate your own cartoons, and play with streams of water that shoot out eight feet.

In the National Inventors Hall of Fame, you can follow the creative processes of great inventors such as Thomas Edison, Alfred Nobel, and Henry Timken. Also, you see many important, original innovations such as the first MRI (magnetic resonance imaging) machine, a laser harp, early electric bulbs, and hundreds of others.

Located at 221 S. Broadway, next to the University of Akron campus, Inventure Place is open year around, seven days a week. Hours are: Mon.-Sat. 9:00 AM to 5:00 PM, and Sun. 12:00 noon to 5:00 PM. Admission fees are: Adults $7.50, seniors and children $6.00. Large families can enter for $25.00.

The facility contains a full-service restaurant and a gift shop. Photography, including flash, is permitted. There's plenty of for-pay parking in two nearby decks; it's free if you have your ticket stamped at the Inventure Place front desk.

For further details, phone: 330-762-4463. Fax: 330-762-6313. Website: www.invent.org.

Akron:
Stan Hywet Hall and Gardens

The largest private residence in Ohio, this elegant, Tudor Revival (English, 16th Century) estate is the dream-child of Franklin Seiberling, co-founder with his brother Charles of the Goodyear Tire & Rubber Co.

Built between 1912 and 1915, the "country home" has 65,000 sq. ft. of floor space on three floors. Furnished with a mixture of 18th, 19th, and 20th Century furniture and decorations -- a combination of antiques and repro-ductions -- the mansion contains 65 rooms, including 18 bedrooms, 25 bathrooms, 273 doors plus 20 sets of French doors, and 21,455 panes of glass.

Besides rivaling Cornelius Vanderbilt's Biltmore chateau for size and opulence, Seiberling's Stan Hywet Hall includes many interesting features and surprises for the visitor. Ex-amples: a mechanical card-shuffler, concealed central heating system, hidden private phone system, and a huge swimming pool in the basement. Also notable are original oil paintings by the famous English artists Thomas Lawrence, Henry Raeburn, and George Romney.

Originally an estate of over 1,000 acres, the remaining 70 acres are noted for their beauty and color. The grounds of the estate, now a National Historical Landmark, includes several formal gardens, lagoons with aquatic plants, and a number of lanes lined with birch and plane trees.

Stan Hywet Hall and Gardens is open for viewing and guided tours all year long, seven days a week, except on Thanksgiving, Christmas, and New Year's Day. Tours are given every half-hour. Hours open: Jan.31 to March 31 -- 10:00 AM to 4:00 PM, Tues. through Sat.; 1:00 PM to 4:00 PM Sun. April 1 through the first week of Jan. -- 10:00 AM to 4:30 PM, seven days a week. You may tour the grounds on any day between 9:00 AM and 6:00 PM.

Entrance fees for the mansion and gardens are: $8.00 adults, $7.00 seniors, $4.00 children 6-12, under 6 free. For the grounds only: $4.00 adults, $2.00 children 6-12, under 6 free. Special group rates are offered.

Stan Hywet Hall and Gardens is located on Akron's northwest side at 714 N. Portage Path, Akron, Ohio 44303. Easiest access is off W. Market St. (State Route 18), north on Portage Path. There's free parking next to the mansion.

Photography is allowed, but no flash. The facility has a museum shop, seasonal cafe, and greenhouse. Special events are planned for every month of the year.

For further details or a free brochure, call: 330-836-5533. Fax: 330-836-2680. Website: www.stanhywet.org.

Ashland:
Ashland County Historical Museum

This museum is contained in an 1859 Victorian manor house, a carriage house, and a barn. Displayed in the manor house are Victorian furniture, pattern-glass goblets, vinegar cruets, paperweights, toys, clothing, and changing exhibits. The house also displays a turn-of-century kitchen and laundry.

In the carriage house you'll find military artifacts, a 14,000-specimen insect collection, and artifacts left by area Indians, pioneers, and settlers. A new building is to contain offices, a library, archives, and more displays.

The museum is open Apr. 1-Dec. 31, on Wed., Fri., and Sun., 11:00 AM to 4:00 PM; also Jan. 1-Mar. 31, Sun. only, 1:00 PM to 4:00 PM. Closed on major U.S. holidays. Group tours are offered by appointment.

Admission is free; donations accepted. You're allowed to take snapshots. There's free parking on nearby streets and on the museum grounds.

Address: 414 Center St., P.O. Box 484, Ashland, OH 44805. Phone: 419-289-3111.

Ashtabula:
Ashtabula Marine Museum

The local Indians called it "Hash-tah-buh-lah," meaning "river of many fish." Thanks to surveyors working for Moses Cleaveland (sic) in 1794, the settlement and river kept that name. After the river was dredged in 1814, shipbuilding began along the banks. This advanced steel-making in Ohio, Michigan, and New York by providing ore carriers and storage facilities. In the process, Ashtabula Harbor became one of the largest ore and coal terminals in the world.

In keeping with this nautical theme, a large frame building on a bluff overlooking the harbor has been converted into the Great Lakes Marine Museum, including a U.S. Coast Guard Memorial Museum. Together they're called the Ashtabula Marine Museum.

Here you can see about 1,000 photos, models, and arti-facts, mainly concerning the harbor's role in Great Lakes shipping. Highlights include:

 * History of bridges crossing the river in town
 * French-made Fresnel lens from a local lighthouse
 * Photos of the "City of New York," a ship used by Admiral Byrd in a trip to Antarctica in 1938
 * Many old photos of shipbuilding on the river
 * Large model of the "Edmund Fitzgerald," an ore carrier that sank in Lake Superior
 * Working model of a Hulett ore-unloader
 * Fully equipped ship's pilot-house, including radar, from the former steamship "Thomas Walters"

This museum is open from Memorial Day through Sept. 1, on Fri., Sat., Sun., and U.S. holidays. Hours are 1:00 PM to 5:00 PM. There's a gift shop near the front door. You can park free on the street in front, or in a small lot next to the museum.

Photography, including flash, is permitted. Admission is free; donations welcome. Special guided tours can be ar-ranged in advance.

Directions: From I-90, take Rte. 11 north to Rte. 531 (Lake Road East). Turn left on 531 to Lake Ave., about 1.2 miles. Turn right on Lake Ave., go about two blocks to Walnut Blvd. Turn right on Walnut, go to end of street. The museum is on the left.

For further details, write to: Ashtabula Marine Museum, 1071 Walnut Blvd., P.O. Box 2855, Ashtabula, OH 44005. Phone: 440-964-6847.

Aurora:
Aurora Museum

Located in the lower level of the Aurora Historical Society's Memorial Library, this museum commemorates Aurora's beginnings through displays of artifacts, tools, photos, and documents. Especially notable are a pictorial history of Aurora, and a display of early cheesemaking equipment used in the area.

The Aurora Museum is open year around on Tues. and Thurs., 1:00 PM to 4:00 PM. Admission is free. You may take snapshots with or without flash. There's free parking beside and behind the building.

Address: 115 E. Pioneer Trail, Aurora, OH 44202. Phone: 440-562-8131.

Directions: At the intersection of SR 306 and SR 43, look for Pioneer Trail. The museum is in the Library building behind a large gazebo.

Barnesville:
Gay 90's Victorian Mansion

Carved oak fretwork and stairways, brass locks and hinges, and doors, mouldings, and mantels finished in butternut are among the attractions in this 26-room, fully restored, Victorian mansion. Built between 1888 and 1893, this "house museum" and its furnishings show the elegance of grand living as the 19th Century flowed into the 20th.

Of note are the lighting fixtures on the first and second floors. These fixtures are combination gas and electric, quite advanced for their time. Running water for the house came from two 540-gallon tanks on the third floor.

This showcase of Victorian interior design is open May 1 through Nov. 1, on Thurs., Fri., and Sat., from 1:00 PM to 4:00 PM. Special tours can be scheduled for any time. Closed on major U.S. holidays.

Admission is $4.00 for adults and seniors, $1.00 for children 6-18. Children under 6 get in free with an adult. You can arrange special rates for large groups.

Photography, including use of flash, is permitted. There's free parking on nearby streets.

Address: 532 N. Chestnut St., Barnesville, OH 43713. Phone: 616-425-2926 or 616-425-3505.

Directions: From I-70, take Exit 202 for SR 800. Go south five miles to Barnesville. SR 800 becomes N. Chestnut St.

Bath:
Hale Farm and Village

On a scale of one to 10, as Northeast Ohio's pioneers go, Jonathan Hale could easily be ranked as an eight or nine. That's because he didn't merely build a log cabin, clear land, and begin farming. Instead, he bought a cabin already built by a squatter; constructed a substantial, three-story house with bricks he made himself; and helped to start and develop local industries as well as his own 500-acre farming tract.

Born in 1777 in Glastonbury, Connecticut, Hale moved in 1810 to what is now Bath Township, some 30 miles south of the Cuyahoga River's mouth on Lake Erie. Along with family members, he cleared heavily forested bottomland to grow wheat and vegetables. He also built furniture, molded and fired bricks, and aided local artisans in starting pottery and glassware manufacturing enterprises.

Today you can see the lasting fruits of his efforts in a living history village called "Hale Farm and Village." Located near the center of the Cuyahoga Valley National Recreation Area, this 178-acre site contains Hale's original brick farmhouse and some outbuildings. Also located on the site are a working forge shop, working sawmill, log schoolhouse, and an early-1900's sugar house.

Just to the north and east of the brick house are clusters of historic frame houses and other buildings moved here from other sites. Equipped with furniture, utensils, decorations, and implements of the early and middle 19th Century, these buildings collectively give you a broad, detailed insight into country life in Ohio's Connecticut Western Reserve.

One building, constructed in 1851, was moved here and altered to represent a carriage factory. Today it displays some 40 carriages and sleighs of the period.

Brick-makers at Hale Farm and Village demonstrate methods of brick manufacture used for many decades before the Industrial Revolution. In October each year, new bricks are molded and fired in the same ways used by Jonathan Hale and his helpers.

In the farmhouse, nicknamed "Old Brick," costumed staff-members demonstrate the old, traditional methods employed in Northeast Ohio for candle-making and cooking. There is a gift shop in the farmhouse where you can buy a variety of souvenirs, including candles, glassware, and wrought-iron pieces made here.

Hale Farm and Village is open from Memorial Day weekend through Oct. 31, on Tues. through Sat., 10:00 AM to 5:00 PM, and on Sun., 12:00 noon through 5:00 PM. The facility is closed on Mondays. Admission fees: $9.00 adults, $7.50 seniors (60 and over), $5.50 children 6-12. Children under 6 get in free when with an adult. Group rates and guided tours are available with advance registration.

The address of this facility is 2686 Oak Hill Road, P.O. Box 296, Bath, OH 44210. There is ample free parking on-site near the farmhouse. Photography, including use of flash, is permitted. For further details and free literature, phone: 330-666-3711. Fax: 330-666-9497.

Bay Village:
Lake Erie Nature and Science Center

Located in the Huntington Reservation of the Cleveland Metroparks system, this facility is a hybrid between a zoo and a natural history museum. It lets you explore the world of living animals, and learn about stars, fossils, plants, weather, water, habitat, and human environment. One of Cleveland's two planetariums is contained within the Center.

The staff conducts a broad range of programs for people of all ages: guided hikes, outdoor exploration, stargazing, animal study, and many others. Special events are held throughout the year. Especially notable is the Center's large collection of live animals, including American Bald Eagles.

The LENSC is open year around, seven days a week, 10:00 AM to 5:00 PM. Closed on major U.S. holidays.

Admission is free. For certain programs, there are small fees.

Photography, including use of flash, is permitted. There's free parking near the entrance. Special tours, hikes, and programs can be arranged.

Address: 28728 Wolf Rd., Bay Village, OH 44140. Phone: 440-871-2900.

Bay Village:
Rose Hill Museum

In 1810, Joseph Cahoon, his wife Lydia, and their eight children arrived in Dover Township by covered wagon. The first of many Eastern pioneer settlers to come here, they built a log cabin in just four days. Then, over the next few years, the family and its neighbors built a sawmill, grist-mill, barn, and orchard.

In 1818, the Cahoons started a permanent homestead. Called Rose Hill, this house has been restored, along with its east and south wings, which were added in the late 1880's. The furniture and utensils now in the house are authentic and appropriate to the various periods of construction.

Nearby are the Osborne Homestead, built in 1810, and a replica of the original Cahoon log cabin. The Bay Village Historical Society owns and operates all three properties.

The Rose Hill Museum is open every Sunday from 2:00 PM to 4:30 PM. Tours at other times can be arranged by appointment. Admission is free. A shop in the museum sells gifts and mementoes.

Photography, including use of flash, is permitted. There's free parking on the property.

Address: 27715 Lake Rd., Bay Village, OH 44140. Phone: 440-871-7338.

Bedford:
Bedford Hist. Soc. Museum

Now a southern suburb of Cleveland, Bedford has done what many other old, small towns should have done, given the will and funds. They've preserved four buildings dating from the 1800s, and turned one of them into a local museum.

Managed by the Bedford Historical Society, and funded by donations, the buildings include the 1874 Township Hall, now on the National Register of Historic Places. Other preserved structures, all on on the town square, are the 1832 Hezekiah Dunham house, 1892 Baptist church (now a community center), and 1882 train depot.

The museum, housed in the old Township Hall, contains period furniture, local Indian artifacts, local archives, manuscripts, paintings, a railway artifact collection, a collection of memorabilia from the 1876 Centennial Exposition, and a historical reference library.

Activities include guided tours on request, temporary exhibitions, and an annual Strawberry Festival. Museum management allows photography, including use of flash, in any of the buildings and at any event.

The museum is open year around. Hours are: Mon. and Wed., 7:30 PM to 10:00 PM; Thurs. 10:00 AM to 4:00 PM; and the second Sunday of every month, 2:00 PM to

5:00 PM. Admission is free; donations welcome. There is parking on nearby streets and in the museum lot.

For more details, write to: Bedford Historical Society, 30 S. Park St., P.O. Box 46282, Bedford, OH 44146. Tel.: 440-232-0796 or 440-232-3339.

Bellevue:
Historic Lyme Village

Strictly speaking, this attraction should not have been included in this guidebook. Bellevue sits about seven miles west of the western boundary we drew, somewhat arbitrarily, for "Northeast Ohio."

The reason we decided to bend the rule is that Historic Lyme Village is such an outstanding attraction, especially to young people and history buffs such as the author. Nowhere else in Ohio will you find an equally outstanding collection of authentic, historic log buildings, all donated and moved to this 13-acre village since 1976.

Containing a total of 16 buildings, all except one of frame or log construction, the village features not only homes but also barns, workshops, stores, and a church. Especially notable is the Seymour House Museum, built in 1836 and furnished with authentic period artifacts, furniture, and decorations.

Also notable: the Detterman Church, one of two remaining log churches in Ohio; the Cooper General Store, with displays from the early 1900s; and the Lyme Post Office. The Groton Township Hall contains the Post Mark Museum, holding over 600 volumes of post marks, plus stamps, postal artifacts, and memorabilia.

The only brick building on the premises is the John Wright Mansion, built in 1850-52 by an immigrant from England. Three stories tall, with 11.5-ft.-high ceilings on the first two floors, this finely furnished home is listed on the National Register of Historic Homes. The building serves as a "house museum," and contains fine examples of furniture, drapery, wallpaper, woodwork, clothing, and other items from the late 1800's and early 1900's. Notable are col-

32

lections of women's clothing, toys, and dolls, plus an Ediphone and early radios.

Historic Lyme Village is funded by membership dues of the HLV Ass'n., and by donations, entrance fees, gift sales, and fund-raising projects. Displaying 7,000 artifacts, the village lies five miles south of the Ohio Turnpike (I-80) near the intersection of State Routes 4 and 113.

If you're coming from the east on the Turnpike, get off at Exit 6A/110. Go south to SR 113, then continue 1/4-mile south to the new entrance and Visitor Center. The address is 5001 SR 4, P.O. Box 342, Bellevue, OH 44811.

Historic Lyme Village is open for 1.5-hr. guided tours June 1 through Aug. 31, daily except Mon., 1:00 PM to 5:00 PM. Also open Sun. in May and Sept., 1:00 PM to 5:00 PM, and for special private events.

With advance reservations, you may hold weddings, receptions, parties, or picnics in three of the buildings on any specified day of the year.

Admission fees: $7.00 for people 13 and over, $6.00 for seniors, $3.00 for children 6-12, incl. Children under 6 get in free with an adult. In groups of 12 or more, people ages 13-64, incl., get in for $6.00 each.

The village holds special events throughout the year. There's a gift shop on-site. Photography, including use of flash, is allowed. There's free parking on a large visitors' lot.

For more information, write to the address above, or phone: 419-483-4949 or 419-483-6052. Website: www.lymevillage.com.

Berea:
Mahler Museum & History Center

Built in 1854 of Berea sandstone, this two-story building was purchased by the Berea Historical Society, thanks to the generosity of local businessman Otto Mahler, his wife, and many others. The attached History Center was added in 1991 to provide space for offices, storage, a resource center, and handicapped access. The Center also has a large room suitable for special exhibits, luncheons, meetings, and special events.

Furnished in the Victorian style, this historic home -- listed on the National Register of Historic Places -- offers a number of interesting highlights. Among them:

* Kitchen -- antique pantry, icebox, gas conversion stove, tealeaf china, and early telephone
* Dining Room -- Haviland Limoges china, rosewood melodeon, pitcher collection, and fireplace
* McKelvey Room -- furnished as a music room and sitting room; contains Eastlake furniture, a parlor organ, Edison gramophone, pre-Civil War piano, and photos of early Berea
* Foyer -- open stairway, "cranberry-wash" chandelier, pier mirror
* Parlor -- antique furnishings, melodeon, walnut desk, wooden-works clock, marble-topped tables
* Second Floor -- four rooms, including a girl's room with antique toys and rope bed, a library, and parents' bedroom with Eastlake furniture, vintage clothing, and antique wash stand.

The History Center contains a number of permanent exhibits. These include an 1874 bucket-brigade wagon and Berea historical mementos. Two special exhibits are the Gray's Candy Kitchen and the Victorian Mansion Dollhouse. The Kitchen, operated by Otto Mahler, has an antique popcorn machine, soda fountain, chocolate molds, and utensils. The eight-ft.-tall dollhouse in the main meeting room shows details of costumes, furniture, and decorations from the period of 1860 to 1910.

This facility is open for tours May 1 through Nov. 30, Tues. and Sun., by appointment only. The office is open Mon.-Thurs., 2:00 PM to 4:00 PM, for information and research.

Admission is free, but the Society accepts donations. Photography without flash is permitted. You'll find free parking on-site, on nearby streets, and on a nearby city lot.

Address: 118 E. Bridge St., P.O. Box 173, Berea, OH 44017. Phone: 440-243-2541.

Berlin:

Schrock's Amish Farm & Home

Located on the eastern edge of Berlin on SR 39, this museum consists of two Amish houses plus outbuildings. One house is a 150-year-old structure, formerly owned by an Old Order Amish bishop, while the other was a "dawdy's" or grandpa's home. Both contain original Amish appliances such as iceboxes and woodburning stoves, along with Amish decorations, utensils, and oak furniture.

Associated with the two houses are numerous gift shops, an oak-furniture shop and store, and buggy-ride concession. Some items such as quilts and leather goods are made on the premises.

The houses are open Apr. 1-Oct. 31, Mon.-Sat., 10:00 AM to 5:00 PM. Closed Sun., Christmas, New Year's Day, Easter, and Thanksgiving. Open on July 4, Memorial Day, and Labor Day.

Photography, including use of flash, is allowed, but do not photograph the Amish people. There's free parking on the property.

Admission is $3.00 adults, seniors, and youths 13-18; $2.00 children 3-12. Those under 3 get in free.

Address: 4363 SR 39, P.O. Box 270, Berlin, OH 44610. Phone: 330-893-3232. Fax: 330-893-3158.

Bexley:
Bexley Hist. Soc. Museum

This museum celebrates Bexley's past with permanent collections of domestic memorabilia and photos. Also contained in the building is a 150-volume library of history books. Activities include guided museum tours, film showings, gallery talks, and temporary and touring exhibits.

Open year around, on Tues., Wed., and Thurs., 9:00 AM to 12:00 noon, and at other times by appointment. Closed on major U.S. holidays.

Admission is free; donations welcome. Photography, including use of flash, is permitted. You'll find free parking in front and on nearby streets.

Address: 2242 E. Main St., Bexley, OH 43209. Phone: 614-235-8694. Fax: 614-235-3420.

Bolivar:
Fort Laurens State Memorial

Built in 1778, Fort Laurens was the only Continental Army outpost built in Ohio during the Revolutionary War. Harrassed by the British and their Indian allies, the fort was finally abandoned in Aug., 1779.

Today the 81-acre site holds a museum and artifacts found from archaeological digs. In the museum, scenes with lifelike, uniformed mannequins depict the activities of the time. An audio-visual program describes the history of the Revolution, and the campaign involving Fort Laurens.

The museum sits on what was once the fort's west gate. A shallow trench outlines the shape of the original structure. Outside the museum, the Tomb of the Unknown Patriot of the American Revolution honors those who fell here.

The museum, operated by the Ohio Historical Society, is open Memorial Day weekend to Labor Day, 9:30 AM to 5:00 PM on Wed. through Sat., and from 12:00 noon to 5:00 PM on Sun. and holidays. The park is open Apr. 1 – Oct. 31, 9:30 AM to dusk daily.

After Labor Day, you may visit the museum on Sat. from 9:30 AM to 5:00 PM, or Sun. 12:00 noon to 5:00 PM, until the end of Oct.

The museum conducts special events each month from May 1 through Oct. 31. Write or phone for details.

Admission to the museum is $3.00 adults, $2.70 seniors, $1.25 children 6-12. Children under 6 get in free with an adult. Group tours at special rates can be arranged,

There is free parking on the grounds. Photography, including use of flash, is permitted.

Address: 11067 Ft. Laurens Rd., Bolivar, OH 44612. Phone: 800-283-8914 or 330-874-2059.

Brooklyn:
Brooklyn Hist. Soc. Museum

An 11-room house contains furniture, decorations, and artifacts from old Brooklyn Township, founded in 1818. On the grounds, you'll find a log cabin with a summer kitchen and schoolroom. Also on the grounds are a fire-engine display, exhibits of antique tools, and a large herb and perennial garden.

The museum and grounds are open from mid-Apr. to Dec. 1, on Tues., 10:00 AM to 2:00 PM, and on Sun., 2:00 PM to 5:00 PM. Admission is free, but donations are welcome.

You may take snapshots by available light; no flash is allowed. There's free parking on the grounds. Special tours can be arranged. A gift shop in the museum offers souvenirs, handcrafts, and herb products from the garden.

Address: 4442 Ridge Rd., Brooklyn, OH 44144. Phone: 216-749-2804.

Burton:
Century Village

A living history museum, Century Village recreates life in Geauga County from 1798 to about 1900. The village consists of 19 structures, 17 of which were moved here from other sites in the county to Burton Hill, just southeast of Burton's town square.

One popular highlight of the collection is the Hickox Brick House. Containing a collection of over 9,000 toy soldiers, the house was built in 1838 by Eleazer Hickox.

The blacksmith shop, built in 1822, was moved here from Auburn Township, and was restored in 1952. The original tools and forge of the 1820s are on display.

Also open for inspection is the Cook House, oldest frame house in Geauga County. Built in 1806, it is furnished as a farmhouse. Many of the original furnishings and utensils can be viewed.

Century Village is open May 1 to Oct. 31, Tues.–Fri., 10:30 AM to 3:00 PM, and on Sat. and Sun., 1:00 PM to 3:00 PM. You can arrange for special tours and group tours with advance reservations.

The facility holds special events throughout the year. For the second half of 1999, these include: Antique Show, July 10; Car Show and Ice Cream Social, July 11; Antique Power Exhibition, July 24 and 25; World War II Remembrance, Aug. 7 and 8; Revolutionary War Remembrance, Sept. 11 and 12; Apple Butter Festival, Oct. 9 and 10; and Haunted Village event, Oct. 23 and 24.

There's a gift shop in the building called Crossroads Store, which offers jams, jellies, giftware, apple butter, maple syrup, and other gifts, many locally made. You can have them packaged and shipped anywhere in the world.

Photography, including use of flash, is allowed. You'll find ample parking on the property and nearby streets.

Admission: $5.00 adults, seniors, and teens; $3.00 children 6–12. Children under 6 get in free with an adult.

For further details, write to: Century Village, P.O. Box 153, Burton, OH 44021. Phone or fax: 440–834–4012. For tours, call: 440–834–1492.

Cambridge:
Cambridge Glass Museum

Founded in 1973, this museum specializes in locally made glassware and pottery. The collections include over 5,000 pieces of Cambridge glass made between 1901 and 1958, and over 100 pieces of Cambridge art pottery. Mr. and Mrs. Harold D. Bennett own and operate the facility.

Open June 1 to Nov. 1, Mon.–Sat., 1:00 PM to 4:00 PM. Closed on Sun. and major U.S. holidays. Admission is $2.00 adults; children get in free. Tours of 10 people or more are charged at $1.00 a person. The museum offers discounts to seniors and AAA members.

A gift shop on the premises profers a variety of glass objects and other souvenirs and gift items.

No photography allowed. There's free parking in front and on nearby streets.

Address: 812 Jefferson Ave., Cambridge, OH 43725. Phone: 740-432-3045.

Cambridge:
Degenhart Paperweight and Glass Museum

Founded in 1978, this museum displays a large collection of 20th Century paperweights, Ohio Valley and Midwest pattern glass, blown and cut artglass objects, and other glass items. The museum has a research library and gift shop.

Open year around. Hours are: Apr. 1–Dec. 31, Mon.–Sat., 9:00 AM to 5:00 PM, Sun. 1:00 PM to 5:00 PM; also Jan. 1–Mar.31, Mon.–Fri., 10:00 AM to 5:00 PM. Closed on major U.S. holidays.

Group tours can be arranged. No photography allowed. There is free parking in front of the building.

Special events include lectures and slide shows about glass production and art.

Admission: $1.50 adults, $1.00 seniors and AAA members. Children 18 and under get in free. Groups of 10 or more are free, too.

Address: 65323 Highland Hills Rd., P.O. Box 186, Cambridge, OH 43725. Phone: 614-432-2626.

Directions: From I-77, get off at Exit 47 onto U.S. 22.

Cambridge:
Guernsey County Museum

Located in the McFarland Home, built in 1831, this is a general historic museum for the county. The Guernsey County Historical Society administers the facility.

Collections on display include historic glassware, china, military items, pottery, hand tools, furniture, kitchen appliances, and others. The "Guernsey County Hall of

Fame" room features photo-engraved plaques honoring 32 former citizens.

Special events staged at the museum include quilt shows and slide shows featuring local and area history. Guided tours are available with advance notice.

The museum is open May 1 to Labor Day, Tues.–Fri. and Sun., 1:30 PM to 5:00 PM; also open Oct. 1–Apr. 30, Tues.–Fri., 1:30 PM to 5:00 PM. Open at other times by appointment. Closed on major U.S. holidays.

Admission: Adults $1.00, children 50 cents. Photography, including use of flash, is permitted. There's free parking on the street in front.

Address: 218 N. 8th St., P.O. Box 741, Cambridge, OH 43725. Phone: 740-439-5884.

SECTION 2 -- CANAL FULTON THROUGH CLEVELAND

Canal Fulton:
Canal Fulton Heritage Soc. Museums

Owned and operated by the Canal Fulton Heritage Society,
this cluster consists of three buildings. They are the Old
Canal Days Museum, 1847 Oberlin House, and 1870's
Heritage House Museum. The Heritage House and Old Canal
Days Museum are open seven days a week, June 1 through
Labor Day, 12:30 PM to 4:30 PM. Closed on major U.S.
holidays.

The museum buildings contain collections of historic furnishings, artifacts from the Ohio & Erie Canal (which ran
through Canal Fulton), and many photos and maps from
canal days. The historic Oberlin House is open by appointment only.

Another attraction that you will enjoy is a ride on a
mule-drawn canal boat, on a restored section of canal. The
"Helena III" operates during June, July, and Aug., seven
days a week, at 1:00, 2:00, and 3:00 PM. The ride costs
$6.50 adults, $5.50 seniors, and $4.50 children.

Photography, including use of flash, is permitted. There's
free parking on the museum grounds and near the boat dock.
Address: 103 Tusacarawas St., Canal Fulton, OH 44614.
Phone: 800-HELENA3.

Canal Winchester:
Mid-Ohio Historical Museum

Housed in a large brick building, this museum is comprised
of seven different exhibit rooms plus a gift shop and lobby.
The specialty here is dolls and toys, including hundreds of
dolls spanning 200 years in the U.S. and Europe. The
collection contains antiques and collectibles; among them are
the original Dionne Quintuplet dolls, Shirley Temples, the
first Barbie, WPA dolls, and rare specimens from France,
Germany, and other countries.

The toy collections contain cast-iron and tin specimens, a large Lionel train exhibit, a complete miniature circus, and others. The gift shop offers old and new collectible dolls. In addition, the staff performs doll repairs, and buys old dolls and toys for the museum.

This museum is open Apr. 1–Dec. 15, Wed.–Sat., 11:00 AM to 5:00 PM. Closed Sun.–Tues. and major U.S. holidays. You can schedule a group tour by making an advance registration.

Admission is $3.00 for people 6 and older; under 6 get in free with an adult. Photography is allowed in some areas (check with your tour guide). There's free parking on the premises.

Address: 700 Winchester Pike, Canal Winchester, 43110. Phone: 614–837–5573.

Canfield:
Loghurst Farm Museum

A living history museum, Loghurst is a three-story log farmhouse built in 1805 by Conrad Neff, a settler from Pennsylvania. Located just outside Canfield on the old Pittsburgh Road (now SR 224, the Boardman–Canfield Rd.) in the Mahoning Valley, the house and farm are fine examples of homesteads that settlers carved out of wooded wilderness. The Western Reserve Historical Society, Cleveland, administers the museum.

Here you can see the evolution of farm life over a century and a half in Northeast Ohio. For example, orginally Mrs. Neff drew water in buckets from an outdoor well, made clothes by hand, cooked meals in a homemade brick fireplace, and worked at night by candlelight. By the early 1900s, though, the wife of the new owner -- Mrs. Ina Kyle -- enjoyed a wood and coal stove, bought many groceries at a local store, and lit the parlor with kerosene lamps.

Today, Loghurst's kitchen shows conditions and implements of the late 1800's and early 1900's. The panelled dining room and Victorian parlor show an elegance achieved by successful, discriminating owners.

Loghurst is open six days a week from May 1 through Oct. 31. Hours are: Tues.–Sat. 10:00 AM to 5:00 PM, Sun. 12:00 noon to 5:00 PM. Closed Mon.

Admission fees: adults $3.00, seniors and children $2.00. Photography, including use of flash, is permitted. There's free parking next to the museum.

For more details, write to: Loghurst Farm Museum, 3967 Boardman–Canfield Rd., Canfield, OH 44046. Phone: 330–533–4330.

Directions: From I–90, go to Rte. 11, turn south to SR 224. Turn left (east), go one mile. The museum is on the right (south) side of SR 224.

Canton:
Canton Classic Car Museum

Located in west–central Canton, just off I–77, this 20,000-sq.-ft. facility was once the second–oldest Ford dealership in the U.S. The original occupants built bicycles and assembled Model T Fords on the second floor. The company also invented the "Hydro-Car," an ill-fated amphibian developed for use in World War I.

In 1994, the museum became a non-profit organization, with funding from the previous owner's family and gifts from outside sources.

Now on display are autos and auto memorabilia from 1904 to 1981. The classic cars range from a 1907 Renault and a 1911 Rolls Royce Silver Ghost, to Johnny Carson's 1981 stainless steel DeLorean. Other interesting cars include a 1932 Packard V-12 hearse, a 1932 Marman V-16 Victoria, a 1970 Plymouth Super Bird, and a 1978 Ferrari sports car.

The facility is renowned for its collection of auto memorabilia, a 1930's gas station, and a display area about the Lincoln Highway. All exhibits are permanent or on long-term loan.

You can have your photo taken behind old-fashioned cutouts, try on vintage hats, ride old arcade rides, or play a jukebox. The museum stages single-marque cruise-ins during the summer, a road tour, and a car show. Check the museum for dates and times.

The Canton Classic Car Museum is open every day, year around, from 10:00 AM to 5:00 PM, but is closed on Thanksgiving, Christmas, New Year's Day, and Easter Sunday. Admission: $5.00 adults, $3.00 seniors, $2.50 children 6-18. Children under 6 get in free with an adult. You can arrange for group rates by phone or mail.

Photography, including use of flash, is permitted. There's parking next to the museum and on the street.

Directions: From I-77, take the 6th Street exit east to Market Ave. The address is Market Ave. and 6th St. SW, Canton, OH 44702. For more information, drop a letter or card, or phone: 330-455-3603. Fax: 330-456-4256.

Canton:
Canton Museum of Art

Founded in 1935, this museum has a permanent collection that focuses on 19th and 20th Century American watercolors and works on paper, and on contemporary ceramics. The museum also shows touring exhibits. Especially popular in recent years have been touring exhibits of works by Andrew Wyeth and Norman Rockwell.

The museum gift shop offers a variety of books, prints, posters, cards, ceramic objects, and other items. Special events during the year include a Christmas art and crafts market, antique show, and pottery-making demonstrations. Call or write for details.

The museum is open year around, Tues.-Sat., 10:00 AM to 5:00 PM; Tues., Wed., and Thurs., 7:00 PM to 9:00 PM; and Sun., 1:00 PM to 5:00 PM. Closed on Mon. and major U.S. holidays.

Admission is $2.50 adults, $1.50 seniors and children. No photography allowed. There is ample parking nearby; most of it is free.

Address: 1001 Market Ave. North, Canton, OH 44702.
Phone: 330-453-7666. Fax: 330-452-4477.

Canton:
McKinley Museum

Administered by the Stark County Historical Society, the museum grounds include the McKinley National Memorial, which contains the tomb of President William McKinley and his family. Also on the 26-acre tract are the McKinley Museum, a general museum containing McKinley memorabilia; a planetarium; a library; and "Discover World," an interactive science gallery.

A highlight of the general museum is simulation of a historic town, with 15 life-size stores and offices. These are authentically furnished after the period 1790 to 1930. This area also contains a 90-ft. historic HO-gauge train exhibit.

Special events at the facility include a "100 Years of Bridal Fashion" show, "Space Week," and "McKinley Day." Check with the museum for dates and times.

Photography, including use of flash, is allowed in Discover World, but not in the historical galleries. There's a gift shop in the general museum offering historic souvenirs and other gifts.

Admission fees are: adults $6.00, seniors $5.00, and children 3 to 18, $4.00. Children under 3 get in free. Group rates are available.

The museum is open year around, seven days a week. Hours are: Mon.-Sat., 9:00 AM to 5:00 PM (to 6:00 PM in summer); on Sun., 12:00 noon to 5:00 PM (to 6:00 PM in summer). Closed on major national holidays.

Directions: From I-77 going south, get off at Exit 106 east. Go left on 13th St. to bottom of hill, take first right to parkway leading to museum. From I-77 going north, use Exit 105, follow signs to museum. There is free parking in lots near the buildings.

For further details, write to: McKinley Museum, 800 McKinley Monument Drive NW, Canton, OH 44708. Phone: 330-455-7043. Fax: 330-455-1137. Website: www.mckinleymuseum.org.

Canton:
National First Ladies' Library

Located in the Victorian-style Saxton-McKinley home in downtown Canton, this facility houses books, newspapers, and other printed materials relating to the lives of our nation's first ladies. Some of the material also relates to social movements and political policies they espoused.

Originally the home of our 25th first lady, Ida Saxton McKinley, the structure has been restored with much attention to historical accuracy. The third-floor ballroom features photos and information about 43 women who served as first ladies or hostesses in the White House.

Rooms open for viewing include President William McKinley's study, Ida McKinley's sitting room, and the main parlor, now a reading room.

The library is open year around, Wed. and Sat., 10:00 AM to 2:00 PM. Admission is $5.00 a person; be sure to make reservations. There's parking on nearby streets and lots. No picture-taking allowed indoors.

Address: 331 Market Ave. South, Canton, OH 44702. Phone: 330-452-0876.

Canton:
Pro Football Hall of Fame

Opened in 1963, this five-building, 83,000-sq.-ft. complex dramatically shows the history of professional U.S. football, honors Hall of Fame members, and displays player and team memorabilia of the National Football League and other, former leagues.

In a 1995 addition, a turntable theater with 20-ft. x 42-ft. Cinemascope screen presents NFL action films. In another theater, a different NFL action film is shown every hour. The Pro Football Photo-Art Gallery displays award-winning still photos from the Hall's annual professional photography contest.

Two large galleries hold niches honoring people who have been enshrined in the Hall of Fame. A Mementos Room displays memorabilia on enshrined players and coaches from the various teams. A photography display with captions tells the history of pro football.

Other attractions include a gift shop and snack shop, plus interactive photo displays and videos that tell the history of football. Each year in late July or early August, the Hall of Fame inducts new members, and stages a parade and AFC-NFC Hall of Fame Game. This is held in Fawcett Stadium, across the street from the facility.

The Hall of Fame is open year around, every day except Christmas. From Memorial Day to Labor Day, hours are 9:00 AM to 8:00 PM. Hours for the remainder of the year are 9:00 AM to 5:00 PM.

Admission: $10.00 adults, $6.50 seniors over 62, $5.00 children 6-14. Younger children get in free with an adult. Large families pay $22.00 max., and reduced rates are available for groups of 25 or more.

Photography, including use of flash, is permitted through-out the facility. There's free parking nearby.

The Pro Football Hall of Fame is located at 2121 George Halas Drive NW, Canton, OH 44708. Phone: 330-456-8207. Fax: 330-456-8175. Website: www.profootballhof.com.

Directions: Off I-77, take Exit 107A. Signs lead you to the parking lot.

Carrollton:
McCook Civil War Museum

Located in the McCook House, built in 1837, this museum specializes in artifacts of local history, Civil War artifacts and memorabilia, antique medical instruments, locally made pottery, and historic textiles. The Carroll County Historical Society administers the facility.

Guided tours for school classes and other groups are available with advance notice. A gift shop in the facility offers a variety of items.

The museum is open from Memorial Day through mid-October, Fri. and Sat., 9:00 AM to 5:00 PM, and on Sun. 1:00 PM to 5:00 PM. Open at other times for tours, by appointment.

Admission: $3.00 adults, $2.50 seniors and AAA members, $1.00 children. Those under 6 get in free with an adult.

Photography, including use of flash, is permitted. There's free parking on nearby streets.

Address: Public Square, P.O. Box 174, Carrollton, OH 44615. Phone: 330-627-3345 or 800-600-7172.

Cleveland:
African American Museum

This museum is said to contain the largest collection of African artifacts in Cleveland. Coming mostly from West and Central Africa, the artifacts include carved wooden masks and statuettes, ceremonial clothing, headdresses, weapons, pottery, musical instruments, and a hut.

The museum is open year around on Tues.–Fri., 10:00 AM to 3:00 PM, and Sat., 11:00 AM to 3:00 PM. Closed on Sun., Mon., and major U.S. holidays.

Admission is $4.00 adults, $3.50 seniors, $3.00 children 4–18. Children under 4 get in free with an adult. Group tours can be arranged with advance registration; tour-groups are charged a fee. Call for details.

No photography is allowed. There's free parking on a lot next to the museum.

Address: 1765 Crawford Rd., Cleveland, OH 44106. Phone: 216-791-1700. Fax: 216-791-1774.

Cleveland:
Cleveland Center for Contemporary Art

Opened in 1968, this 20,000-sq.-ft. art museum always contains a variety of rotating exhibits of contemporary paintings, sculpture, and other forms of fine art. The museum shows 12 exhibitions a year.

Housed on the second floor of the Cleveland Play House building, with three galleries and a cafe, the museum is open year around, six days a week. Hours are: Tues.-Thurs. 11:00 AM to 6:00 PM, Fri. 11:00 AM to 9:00 PM, Sat. and Sun. 12:00 noon to 5:00 PM. Closed Mon.

Admission is free at all times. There is for-pay, guarded parking on the site. You're allowed to take snapshots, with or without flash.

For more details, write to: Cleveland Center for Contemporary Art, 8501 Carnegie Ave., Cleveland, OH 44106. Phone: 216-421-8671. Fax: 216-421-0737.

Cleveland:
Cleveland Museum of Art

Opened in 1916, this museum is regarded by some experts to be one of the top 10 art museums in the U.S. Expanded several times, it contains over 34,000 works of fine art in many media.

Paintings, sculpture, tapestries, pottery, photo prints, and other works from the same period are grouped together in galleries on three floors. The Lower Level shows art from Asia, and contains changing exhibits, a lecture hall, and a recital hall. Level 1 contains exhibits of contemporary photos and Asian, Pre-Columbian, and Native American arts, plus an outdoor sculpture garden, auditorium, and a large hall for traveling exhibitions. The main lobby is on this level.

Level 2 contains numerous galleries showing art from the Ancient Near East, Egypt, Greece, and Rome; the Middle Ages; and Modern Europe and America. One outstanding exhibit is the newly remodeled Armor Court, containing numerous weapons and suits of armor from Medieval and Renaissance Europe.

Major traveling exhibitions are conducted several times a year. Watch your newspaper and TV news for publicity about these events.

The museum is open year around. Hours are: Tues., Thurs., Sat., and Sun. 10:00 AM to 5:00 PM; Wed. and Fri. 10:00 AM to 9:00 PM. Closed on Mon. and major U.S. holidays.

The building contains a cafe and several gift shops on Level 1. Photography is permitted for certain permanent exhibits, but no flash or tripods allowed. Check at the desk regarding what you want to photograph.

Admission is free, but sometimes there's a charge to see major traveling exhibitions. These may also require reservations. The museum has its own parking lot and deck next to the building, offering for-pay, guarded parking. There's also free and metered parking on nearby streets.

Address: 11150 East Blvd., University Circle, Cleveland, OH 44106. Phone: 216-421-7350 or 888-CMA-0033. Website: www.clemusart.com.

Cleveland:
Cleveland Museum of Natural History

A gallery of gemstones and jewels, the "Planet e" Hall of Earth and Planetary Exploration, and a tour of Ohio's rocks and rock formations: these are among the permanent exhibits you'll find at The Cleveland Museum of Natural History in University Circle.

Long known for its fine collection of dinosaur skeletons, this 200,000-sq.-ft. facility offers interesting exhibits about Native Americans, wild animals, fossils, prehistoric Man, Middle America, plants, and other aspects of life on earth.

The museum has a hands-on discovery center, planetarium and observatory, and gift shop. Special tours, classes, and field trips can be arranged. You can even see live wild animals in the museum's own little zoo.

The facility is open year around, seven days a week, except on major U.S. holidays. Hours are: Mon.-Sat., 10:00 AM to 5:00 PM; Sun., 12:00 noon to 5:00 PM. During Sept.-May, the museum is open on Wed. evenings to 10:00 PM.

Admission is $6.50 adults, $4.50 seniors and students 5-17. Children 4 and under get in free with an adult. Ask about special group tours and rates.

Photography, including use of flash, is permitted. You'll find for-pay parking on a lot in front of the museum, and metered or free parking on nearby streets.

Directions: From Euclid Ave., drive north on East Blvd. to Wade Oval Drive. Turn left. The address is: 1 Wade Oval Dr., Cleveland, OH 44106. Phone: 216-231-4600. Toll-free: 800-317-9155. Website: www.cmnh.org.

Cleveland:
Cleveland Police Hist. Soc. Museum

Thanks to an old TV series, many of us know that Eliot Ness helped to bring down Chicago mob-boss Al Capone in the early 1930's. Were you aware, however, that after Ness's success in Chicago, Cleveland appointed him as the city's Director of Safety, beginning in 1935?

A display on Ness's achievements, including his years in Cleveland, is one of the exhibits at the Cleveland Police Museum. Established in May, 1983, its 1,300 sq. ft. of floor space -- plus seven display cases in the lobby -- illustrate and describe many interesting aspects of years-ago law enforcement in the city.

Along with the Cleveland Police Historical Society, Inc., a non-profit organization, the museum is located on the first floor of police headquarters, one block north of Public Square.

Among the highlights are a book of thieves (1887-1891), a 1920 jail cell and fingerprinting table, death masks from the 1935 torso murders at Kingsbury Run, early polygraphs, an assortment of firearms, and CPD Harley-Davidson motorcycles from 1960 and 1973.

The museum is open year around, Mon.-Fri., 10:00 AM to 4:00 PM. Admission is free. There is parking on the street and in nearby commercial lots and garages. No photography allowed. You can arrange for guided tours by advance registration.

For further details, write to: Cleveland Police Historical Society, Inc., and Museum, 1300 Ontario St., Cleveland, OH 44113. Phone: 216-623-5055. Fax: 216-623-5145.

Cleveland:
Cleveland State Univ. Art Gallery

This 4,500-sq.-ft. gallery was founded by the University's Art Department faculty in 1973. It is funded by student fees and grants from the Ohio Arts Council.

Comprised of one large space and several smaller spaces, the gallery specializes in contemporary paintings, photo- graphs, sculpture, and other forms of the fine arts. Con- tributors to the exhibits include CSU art students, Cleveland-area artists, and artists of national and international reputation.

The gallery often puts on thematic group shows. Largest of these is the biannual "People's Art Show," which is totally open to exhibitors without fees and without jury judgments.

There's no charge for admission to the gallery. Management allows photography, including use of flash, provided the photos are not for commercial use. You'll find ample parking on a visitor lot at E. 24th St. and Euclid Ave., and metered parking on nearby streets.

The CSU Art Gallery is open year around, six days a week, Mon.-Fri. 10:00 AM to 5:00 PM, Sat. 12:00 noon to 4:00 PM. Closed on Sun. For more information, write to the gallery at 2307 Chester Ave., Cleveland, OH 44114. Phone: 216-687-2103. Fax: 216-687-9340.

Cleveland:
Crawford Auto-Aviation Museum

If you like automobiles, including antique, vintage, and classic cars, you'll find a veritable "candy store" in the 75,000-sq.-ft. Crawford Auto-Aviation Museum.

Now boasting nearly 200 antique, vintage, and classic models, this venue consistently scores in the Top Five among U.S. auto museums. Stars of the show include an 1897 Panhard-et-Levassor, and a 1909 Sears "mail-order" car priced at $395.

Founded in 1937 by Frederick C. Crawford, former president of Thompson Products Co. (a pioneer maker of auto and airplane parts), the museum's collection now includes over 175 vintage autos and eight airplanes on exhibit. Among the outstanding specimens in the collection is the 1897 Panhard-et-Levassor. Built in Paris, France, this is the oldest auto in the Crawford collection, and the only known closed specimen still in existence.

Panhard-et-Levassor was the first automaker to move the engine from under the front seat to the front of the car, under a hood. Also the first company to build a series of autos, Panhard-et-Levassor sold out in 1965 to Citroen. Their original two-seater sold for the equivalent of $1,130.

Another attraction is a 1904 steam-powered Model D touring car from the White Sewing Machine Co., Cleveland, Ohio. Burning kerosene or gasoline, this car's boiler generated steam which drove four pistons.

At the 1901 New York Automobile Show, visitors saw 58 brands of steamers, 23 electrics, and 58 gasoline internal-combustion models. By the 1905 show, only nine steamers had survived competition.

Cleveland's White Sewing Machine Co. built 719 Model D's in 1904. Later on, the company became the White Motor Co., and specialized in building trucks.

The lowest-priced model here is a 1909 Sears Motor Buggy. Listing at $395 at the factory, this two-cylinder, air-cooled, 12-hp model had a double direct chain-drive.

Chicago-based Sears sold the gasoline-powered Motor Buggy by catalog, shipping to railroad freight terminals all across the nation. According to a museum placard, this model was especially popular in remote rural areas, which had no city-type dealers.

There are many other attractions in the collection, including early Fords, an 1899 Winton, 1900 Benz, 1903 Cadillac Model A, 1905 Stanley Steamer, and 1914 Peerless Model 60.

Fans of more recent models will appreciate the 1928 Rolls Royce Phaeton, 1937 Cord, 1956 Chevrolet Convertible, 1973 Ford Mustang Convertible, and 1981 Aston Martin Lagonda. In the racing-car category, recent acquisitions include a 1982 March C2 Indy, Vega Formula Vee, and Argo JM-2 Super Vee.

Located in the Western Reserve Historical Society complex at 10825 East Blvd., Cleveland, the Crawford is open year around from 10:00 AM to 5:00 PM Mon. through Sat., and 12:00 noon through 5:00 PM on Sun. Admission is $6.50 for adults, $5.50 for seniors, and $4.50 for students. Photography, including flash, is permitted. There's for-pay parking in a lot behind the museum.

For more details, phone: 216-721-5722.

Cleveland:
Dittrick Museum of Medical History

This museum contains nearly 75,000 objects of interest relating to the history of medicine, surgery, dentistry, and pharmacy. Emphasis is on Cleveland and the Western Reserve. Of particular note are exhibits of a 19th-Century doctor's saddlebag and instruments, a Western Reserve pharmacy of the late 1800's, a reconstructed 19th-Century doctor's office, surgical instruments from the 1800's, and a historical sequence of microscopes showing their development.

One of the largest collections of its kind in the U.S., this one is said to lead in the number of specimens of equipment for surgical technology and gastrointestinal endoscopy.

The Dittrick Museum is on the third floor of the Allen Memorial Library building at the corner of Euclid Ave. and Adelbert Rd. in University Circle. Open year around, Mon.–Fri. 10:00 AM to 5:00 PM. Closed on weekends and major holidays.

Admission is free, but there's a small charge for group tours. Photography, including use of flash, is permitted. You can park on nearby streets.

Address: 11000 Euclid Ave., Cleveland, OH 44106. Phone: 216–368–3648. Fax: 216–368–0165.

Cleveland:
Dunham Tavern Museum

Once a stagecoach stop on the old Buffalo–Cleveland–Detroit post road, Dunham Tavern Museum is the oldest building still standing on its original site in Cleveland. Today the property extends a full block, and is listed on the National Register of Historic Places. It is also designated a Cleveland Landmark.

Rufus and Jane Pratt Dunham arrived in the Western Reserve from Massachusetts in 1819. They lived in a log cabin until the first part of the house was built in 1824. Mr. Dunham, a tavernkeeper and farmer, used the home as a social and political center. In 1857, the house was sold to a local banker, and it served as a residence through the rise and decline of "Millionaire's Row" on Euclid Ave. and the rapid growth of Cleveland.

Inside the museum are many items of early Americana. A formal parlor is furnished in the style of Western Reserve settlers from Connecticut. The original taproom and "ladies' parlor" preserve the atmosphere of a meeting place of the mid–1800's. Other rooms are furnished with 19th–Century antiques.

Special events at this facility include lectures and outdoor festivals. On the grounds outside you'll find a historic log cabin and, in season, an herb garden.

The museum is open year around, Wed. and Sun., 1:00 PM to 4:00 PM. Closed on major U.S. holidays. Guided tours for groups can be arranged with advance notice.

Admission: $2.00 adults, seniors, and youths 12-18; and $1.00 children under 12.

Photography, including use of flash, is permitted. There's free parking on the museum grounds.

Address: 6709 Euclid Ave., Cleveland, OH 44103. Phone: 216-431-1060. Website: www.logan.com/tavern.

Cleveland:
Great Lakes Science Center

This is a hands-on, educational museum, with emphasis on science, the environment, and current technologies. Floor space totals 165,000 sq. ft. Funding is largely from private, corporate, and foundation gifts, and from admission fees.

One outstanding exhibit is the Great Lakes Situation Room, which features the largest video wall east of the Rockies. The Environmental Floor houses the largest exhibit anywhere on the Great Lakes. Also in this building is the Cleveland Clinic Omnimax Theater, the only one of its kind in this region.

Altogether there are over 300 interactive, permanent exhibits, plus a number of traveling exhibits, on three floors. Staffers conduct demonstrations, science experiments, and lectures each day. The Science Store offers a wide selection of educational items, books, models, and souveniers.

The Great Lakes Science Museum is open every day, year around, except on Thanksgiving and Christmas. Hours are 9:30 AM to 5:30 PM.

A new parking facility next to the museum offers for-pay parking. A covered walkway connects the two structures. Parking here costs $5.00 for guests of the Science Center.

Photography, including use of flash, is allowed throughout the museum, but not in the theater. Admission fees for museum plus theater: $10.95 adults, $9.95 seniors, $7.75 children 3-17. For seniors, museum-only or theater-only costs $6.75. For adults or children, admission to one but not the other costs $7.75 adults, $5.25 children.

Address: 601 Erieside Ave., Cleveland, OH 44114. This is at the northern end of E. 9th St., at the Pier.

For further details, including show-times and theater reservations, phone: 216-694-2000. Fax: 216-696-2140. (Reservations for the theater are recommended.)

Cleveland:
Health Museum of Cleveland

Want to see what's inside a human body? See "Juno the Talking Transparent Woman" at the Health Museum of Cleveland. Made of clear plastic parts, this transparent model shows internal organs, bones, nerves, and blood vessels realistically.

Juno is one of many interesting exhibits relating to health, anatomy, and health science education at this museum. Founded in 1936, the 20,000-sq.-ft. facility was the first of its kind in the Western Hemisphere, and is now one of only six in the U.S.

Another popular exhibit is "The Giant Tooth," an 18-ft., two-ton replica of a molar. Fourteen satellite displays explain dental health and orthodontic care.

A relatively new exhibit called "Come to Your Senses" explores the five senses of smell, sight, hearing, taste, and touch, explaining how they work.

All-told, there are 150 permanent exhibits in the museum, and often one or more special or traveling exhibits. Many are interactive. The museum holds special events throughout the year; for dates and times, get in touch with their office. Also, you can rent the museum space for birthdays and other special events.

Photographing certain exhibits is permitted, but no flash. (To find out what you may photograph, check at the desk.) There's free parking next to the building. Admission is $4.50 adults, $3.00 seniors and students with ID, free to children under 3 with an adult. Group rates are offered.

The museum is open year around, seven days a week, except on major national holidays. Hours are: Mon.-Fri.

9:00 AM to 5:00 PM, Sat. 10:00 AM to 5:00 PM, Sun. 12:00 noon to 5:00 PM.

Address: 8911 Euclid Ave., Cleveland, OH 44106. Phone: 216-231-5010. Fax: 216-231-5129. Website: www.healthmuseum.org.

Cleveland:
Int'l. Women's Air & Space Museum

Located in the Burke Lakefront Airport Terminal, this museum is dedicated to preserving the history of women in aviation and space, and to documenting their continuing contributions. The museum moved here from Centerville, opening to the public in Aug., 1999. Exhibits feature:

* Harriet Quimby, first woman to fly the English Channel, 1912

* Katherine Wright, sister of Orville and Wilbur

* Amelia Earhart and other pioneering female aviators

* Women's roles in World War II Army and Navy aviation, and in commercial aviation

* Jacqueline Cochran (U.S.) and Jacqueline Auriol (France), pioneers in high-speed jet flying

* Women in space programs of the U.S. and USSR

This museum is open daily, year around, 10:00 AM to 4:00 PM. Admission is free. There's free and for-pay parking on the airport lot. Photography, including use of flash, is permitted.

A gift shop on the premises offers a variety of aviation-related items. These include books, T-shirts, coffee mugs, medallions, and others.

Address: 1501 N. Marginal Rd., Cleveland, OH 44114, Room 165.. Phone: 216-623-1111. Fax: 216-623-1113. Website: www.iwasm.org.

Cleveland:
Lake View Cemetery

Like Boston, Paris, and other great cities, Cleveland has
cemeteries that qualify as tourist attractions. Most notable
among these is Lake View Cemetery on the city's East Side.

Here you can visit the Pres. James A. Garfield Monument,
a fine architectural specimen, and the Jeptha Wade Memorial Chapel. Designed by Louis Comfort Tiffany, it honors
the founder of the Western Union Telegraph Co. The chapel
boasts a striking, original stained-glass window plus wall
mosaics and marble mosaic floors.

Guided tours of the entire grounds are offered, or you
can use a map to take a self-guided tour. Prominent
Clevelanders buried here include not only Pres. Garfield but
also John D. Rockefeller, Marcus Hanna, the Van Sweringen
brothers, and 21 past mayors.

Other notables interred at Lake View are:

* Charles F. Brush, inventor of the arc lamp and streetcar dynamo

* Leonard Case, Jr., founder of the Case School of
Applied Science

* Dr. George Washington Crile, Sr., who performed the
first successful blood transfusion. He was a founder of the
Cleveland Clinic.

* Dr. Harvey W. Cushing, pioneer brain surgeon and
biographer of Sir William Osler

* John Milton Hay, Pres. Lincoln's private secretary for
four years, and ambassador to Great Britain

* Samuel L. Mather, mining and shipping industry
pioneer, and a founder of the Cleveland Iron Mining Co.,
now Cleveland Cliffs

* Garrett A. Morgan, inventor of a gas mask and the
first three-color electric traffic light

* Alexander Winton, pioneer automaker, known for the
"Winton Six"

In warm months, you'll find it worthwhile to view the
hundreds of marked specimen trees and the flower gardens
in the cemetery.

Lake View's grounds are open year around. The Wade Chapel may be viewed Apr. 1–Oct. 31, and the Garfield Memorial Apr. 1–Nov. 19. Hours are 9:00 AM to 4:00 PM.

Admission is free. Photography, including use of flash, is allowed, provided it is for personal and not commercial use.

Parking on the grounds is free.

Address: 12316 Euclid Ave., Cleveland, OH 44106. Phone: 216-421-2665. Fax: 216-421-2415.

Cleveland:
NASA John Glenn Visitor Center

The National Aeronautics and Space Administration (NASA) operates the John H. Glenn Research Center at Lewis Field southwest of Cleveland, next to Hopkins International Airport. At the Visitor Center, some 8,000 sq. ft. is devoted to a space museum.

Here you can see a real spacecraft, moon rock, astronauts' tools and space suits, and many other artifacts, photo displays, and dioramas pertaining to space exploration and spacecraft. Numerous rockets and missiles are displayed on the grounds outdoors.

The Visitor Center is open year around, Mon.–Fri. 9:00 AM to 4:00 PM, Sat. 10:00 AM to 3:00 PM, Sun. 1:00 PM to 5:00 PM, and on minor holidays 10:00 AM to 3:00 PM. Closed on Christmas Eve, Christmas Day, New Year's Eve, New Year's Day, Easter Sunday, and Thanksgiving.

Admission is free. Tours can be scheduled for Wed. or Sat. Photography, including use of flash, is permitted. There's free parking next to the building.

Address: 21000 Brookpark Rd., Cleveland, OH 44135. Phone: 216-433-2000 or 216-433-9834 (TDD). Website: www.grc.nasa.gov/.

Directions: From I-480 southwest of Cleveland, get off at Exit 9, and go south to Brookpark Rd. (SR 17). The entrance to the John Glenn Research Center is just west of this intersection. Follow signs to the Visitor Center.

60

Cleveland:
**Rock & Roll Hall of Fame
And Museum**

Located on Cleveland's lakefront at the foot of E. 9th St., this facility has 55,000 sq. ft. of exhibit space. It includes displays of personal artifacts from musicians and groups, such as their musical instruments and costumes. Also on display are many paintings, interactive computer databases, and photos pertaining to rock & roll music.

The building contains a 200-seat multi-media theater, cafe, and gift shop. Special activities include concerts, lectures, annual tribute to a music "legend," and annual induction ceremony.

The building is open year around, Mon.-Tues. and Thurs.-Sun. 10:00 AM to 5:30 PM, and Wed. 10:00 AM to 9:00 PM. Closed on major U.S. holidays.

Admission: $14.95 adults and youths 12-18, $11.50 seniors and children 4-11. Children under 4 get in free.

No photography permitted indoors. There is for-pay parking on nearby streets and in parking lots and garages.

Address (mailing): One Key Plaza, Cleveland, OH 44114. Phone: 216-781-7625 or 1-888-764-ROCK. Fax: 216-781-1832.

Cleveland:
Romanian Ethnic Art Museum

The original set of artifacts in this collection were brought to the U.S. in 1923 by Anisoara Stan, a protegee of Queen Marie of Romania. After being exhibited in various parts of the country, the collection was donated to St. Mary's Romanian Orthodox Church of Cleveland. Subsequent donations of artifacts continue to enrich the collection.

Most items here are regional folk costumes notable for their color, unique design, and decorative threads, beads, and sequins. They are worked on handloomed fabric made in Romanian villages. The style of each costume is dictated by regional tradition, but the specific design of each comes from the creativity of the individual seamstress or tailor.

Other artifacts on display include ceramics, carved wood pieces, metalwork, religious icons, sculpture, and paintings on canvas and glass. Ecclesiastical vestments and accessories, along with historical photos and books, round out the collection.

Housed in a hall at St. Mary's Church, the museum is open for guided tours by appointment only. Admission is free, but donations are requested.

You can take snapshots and use flash. There's free parking on the church grounds.

Address: 3256 Warren Rd., Cleveland, OH 44111.

Cleveland:
South Boulevard Historical Society

This private enterprise specializes in exhibiting looms, spinning wheels, cast-iron stoves, Shaker heirlooms, and antique fabrics. Demonstrations of spinning and weaving are given. You can view about 100 items on display.

Photography, including use of flash, is permitted. There's parking on nearby streets. Admission is free; donations welcome. Open by appointment.

Address: 10128 South Blvd., Cleveland, OH 44108. Phone: 216-791-4614. Fax: 216-791-4614. Website: www.southboulevard.org.

Cleveland:
Steamship W.G. Mather Museum

Between 1925 and 1980, this 618-ft.-long bulk-cargo carrier hauled 14,000-ton loads of iron ore from the Mesabi Range near Lake Superior down to Cleveland steel mills. The return trip was used to carry Ohio, W. Va., and Pennsylvania coal back up to Minnesota.

Then, after sitting idle for about 10 years, she was converted into a floating maritime museum, which opened in

May, 1991. Four years later, the American Society for Mechanical Engineers had her declared a National Historic Landmark. That was done partly because she's fitted with an advanced boiler control system and dual-propeller bow thrusters.

Today you can tour this huge ship –– called the Steamship William G. Mather Museum –– and see her cargo holds, pilot house, galley (kitchen), living quarters, and engine room. In all, some 60,000 sq. ft. of deck space are open for touring.

The museum holds special events several times during the year. Visitors can enjoy a one-hour guided tour and a 20-min. videotape on the ship's history. The tour requires climbing steep steps and crossing open decks.

The Mather is open daily from Memorial Day through Labor Day, and on Fri., Sat., and Sun. during May, Sept., and Oct. Hours are 10:00 AM to 5:00 PM Mon.-Sat., and 12:00 noon to 5:00 PM Sun.

Admission fees: $5.00 adults, $4.00 seniors, $3.00 children 5 and up. Those 4 and under get in free with an adult. Group rates are offered.

Parking is available on nearby for-pay lots and decks, and in metered spaces on nearby streets. Photography, including use of flash, is permitted except during copyrighted programs and performances. (Check with your tour guide.)

The Mather is tied next to the E. 9th St. pier. Address: Steamship W.G. Mather Museum, 1001 E. 9th St. Pier, Cleveland, OH 44114. Phone: 216-574-9053. Fax: 216-574-2536.

Cleveland:
Ukrainian Museum and Archives

Located in Cleveland's Tremont neighborhood, this facility contains a broad selection of artifacts, printed records, and artwork pertaining to Ukraine. Included are works of folk-arts and fine-arts, including paintings, sculpture, ceramics, religious vestments, embroidered clothing and textiles, and a permanent exhibit of over 100 hand–painted Easter eggs ("pysansky").

The library contains over 16,000 volumes on topics ranging from pre–historic Ukraine to the present human–rights movement. Numerous volumes pertain to the Diplaced Persons camps after World War II. An unusual item is the 1793 missal in Ukrainian.

The archives contain many current Ukrainian periodicals, pre–Soviet publications, and complete volumes of post–war Svoboda and America, two Ukrainian–language newspapers. A unique feature is the Shevchenko Collection, including over 1,000 books, periodicals, clipping files, and memorabilia about Taras Shevchenko, Ukraine's poet laureate. This is the largest collection of its kind in North America.

The UMA is open year around on Wed. and Thurs., 10:00 AM to 4:00 PM, and by appointment at other times. Admission is free but donations are requested.

You may take snapshots in the museum, with or without flash. There is free parking on nearby streets.

Address: 1202 Kenilworth Ave., Cleveland, OH 44113. Phone: 216–781–4329. Website: www.umacleveland.org.

Directions: From I–90 west, get off at W. 14th St. Go one block on W. 14th to Kenilworth Ave.; turn left. Or, from I–71, take W. 14th St. to Kenilworth Ave, and turn east.

Cleveland:
U.S.S. Cod Submarine Museum

A National Historic Landmark, the U.S.S. Cod is the last completely authentic World War II American submarine in existence. From May 1 through Sept. 30, you can descend a ladder into this historic fighting ship. Almost all the living and fighting quarters are open for your inspection.

Part of a fleet of some 250 U.S. subs, the 90–man Cod sank 6 major enemy vessels and damaged seven others. She also rescued the crew of the grounded Dutch sub O–19, and during the Cold War helped train NATO forces to track Soviet subs.

Open May 1 to Sept. 30, seven days a week, 10:00 AM

to 5:00 PM. Open on July 4 and Labor Day.

Photography, including use of flash, is permitted. There's free parking nearby.

Admission: $4.00 adults, $2.00 students. Guided tours can be arranged.

Address: 1089 E. 9th St., Cleveland, OH 44114. Phone: 216-566-8770. Website: www.usscod.org.

Directions: From I-90, I-71, or I-77, get off downtown at E. 9th St. Take the Marginal Rd. east about 1,000 ft. past the Rock & Roll Hall of Fame and Museum.

(Note: Every visitor must be able to climb vertical ladders, and to enter and exit the submarine.)

Cleveland:
Western Reserve History Museum

One of the nation's top-ranked costume collections, called the Chisholm Halle Costume Wing, may be seen in the Western Reserve Historical Society History museum. The collections are housed in a 1911 mansion designed by the son of President James A. Garfield. Costumes from the late 1700s to the present are on display. Two other buildings complete the museum, which was founded in 1871.

Also on display are drawings and maps made by the survey team headed by Moses Cleaveland (sic), founder and surveyor of Ohio's largest city. Engravings and photos show how the area subsequently grew, with the addition of roads, canals, and railroads. Rotating special exhibits feature topics ranging from football, to the Civil War, to the Shakers. There is a gift shop on the premises.

Special events at the Western Reserve Historical Society Museum include "Family History Days" and the "African-American Heritage and Cultural Celebration."

The museum is open seven days a week, year around. Hours are: Mon.-Sat. 10:00 AM to 5:00 PM, Sun. 12:00 noon to 5:00 PM. Admission fees are: $6.50 adults, $5.50 seniors, $4.50 students. Children under 6 (with an adult) and members of the Western Reserve Historical Society get in free. Group rates and special tours are available with advance reservations.

There's for-pay parking in a lot next to the facility. Photography, including use of flash, is permitted in all display areas except the costume wing.

For more information, write to: WRHS History Museum, 10825 East Blvd., Cleveland, OH 44106. Phone: 216-721-5722. Fax: 216-721-8934.

SECTION 3 -- COLUMBIANA
THROUGH GNADENHUTTEN

Columbiana:
Log House Museum

Located four blocks away from its current site in the
1820's, this house was built by Jacob Nessly. Moved in
1975, the building is now used as a museum and meeting
place by The Historical Society of Columbiana-Fairfield
Township. The Society added an annex in 1978.

On display are items collected by the Society since its
founding in 1953. Included are quilts and coverlets made in
the area in the 1830's, pioneer tools and implements, a few
10,000-year-old mastadon bones found on a nearby farm,
and a collection of mementoes and artifacts from the Civil
War.

The museum is open during June, July, and Aug. on Sat.
and Sun., 2:00 PM to 4:00 PM. Closed on major U.S.
holidays. Group tours can be arranged for days and times
convenient for you.

Admission is free, but the Society welcomes donations.
Photography, including use of flash, is permitted. You'll find
free parking on a church property one building away.

Address: 10 E. Park Ave., Columbiana, OH 44408.
Phone: None; contact by mail.

Columbus:
Center of Science and Industry (COSI)

Now called COSI Columbus, this museum plans to move to
new quarters in Nov., 1999. There is a sister facility in
Toledo called COSI Toledo.

Designed to provide hands-on fun for children, COSI
Columbus reveals the principles, look, and excitement of
physical science through participation. For example, kids
can:

* Jump, stomp, and pound on a platform connected to a
real seismograph, revealing the child's "earthshaking power"

* Learn weather technology, as in the "Toto" data-collecting tool to measure characteristics of tornadoes

* Fly into the eye of a hurricane in the seat of a simulated P-3 weather observation plane.

The museum contains many static displays, too. These include a 16-ft. tree bent 90 degrees by Hurricane Hugo, and ash and debris from the eruption of Mount St. Helens.

Until Nov., 1999, COSI Columbus is at 280 E. Broad St., Columbus, OH 43215. Phone: 614-288-2674. Fax: 614-222-2899. E-mail: COSI @ compuserve.com.

The museum is open year around, Mon.-Sat. 10:00 AM to 5:00 PM, and Sun. 12:00 noon to 5:30 PM. Closed on major U.S. holidays.

Photography, including use of flash, is allowed. There is for-pay parking near the facility.

Admission: $8.00 adults 19-65, $7.00 seniors and students 6-18, $6.00 children 2-12. Children under 2 get in free.

The new COSI Columbus, to be located at 333 W. Broad St., will include a giant-screen theater, domed theater, and two galleries for temporary exhibitions, as well as a restaurant, gift shop, and seven areas for permanent exhibitions. These will be devoted to hands-on learning about the oceans, problem-solving, computers (including games), history of technology, health and science, tools, and space exploration. Being developed in partnership with NASA, the space area will open in late 2000.

After Nov. 1, 1999, call Information in Columbus for the new phone number, hours, fees, etc. Call 614-555-1212.

Columbus:
Columbus Museum of Art

Founded in 1878, this museum has outstanding collections of paintings from the schools of Impressionism and American Modernism, and from contemporary artists. Noted names represented include Degas, Matisse, Monet, Picasso, Cassatt, Bellows, Hopper, and O'Keeffe.

Special features include the Russell Page Sculpture Garden, Ross Photography Center, and an interactive exhibit for
children. Temporary, traveling exhibitions are on display
frequently; these include showings of photographs, paintings,
basketry, porcelain, and other media.

The museum building contains a gift shop and children's
shop, plus a cafe serving lunch and Sunday brunch.

Open year around, six days a week: Tues.–Sun. 10:00
AM to 5:30 PM, Thurs. 10:00 AM to 8:30 PM. Closed on
Mon. and major national holidays.

Admission: $4.00 adults, $2.00 seniors and children 6–
18. Children under 6 get in free. On Thurs. PM, admission
is free to all.

Free tours of featured exhibitions or permanent collections
are offered on most Fridays at noon, and on Sun. at 2:00
PM. Call for details.

Photography of most permanent collections is permitted,
but no flash or tripods allowed. There is parking behind the
museum; it's free to members, $2.00 to others.

Address: 480 E. Broad St., Columbus, OH 43215.
Phone: 614–221–6901; for recorded info., call 614–221–
4848. Website: www.columbusart.mus.oh.us.

Columbus:
Columbus Santa Maria

This is a full–scale, furnished wooden replica of the flag-
ship in Christopher Columbus's 1492 fleet. Ninety–eight ft.
long, it is berthed and open Apr.–Oct. for touring on the
Scioto River, just north of the Broad St. Bridge.

Built from historically accurate plans, the Columbus Santa
Maria presents an accurate portrayal of conditions Columbus
and his crews faced during their momentous voyages to
America. Tour guides are on–hand to explain ship furnishings, construction, and sailing methods.

You may tour the ship June 2–Labor Day, Wed.–Fri.
10:00 AM to 5:00 PM, and Sat.–Sun. 11:30 AM to 6:00
PM. Also open Apr. 10–June 2 and Labor Day to Oct. 31;

hours are Wed.–Fri. 10:00 AM to 3:00 PM, and Sat.–Sun. 12:00 noon to 5:00 PM. Open Memorial Day, July 4, and Labor Day from 12:00 noon to 5:00 PM.

Admission fees are $3.50 adults, $3.00 seniors (60+) ($2.50 in tour groups), and $1.50 youths 5–17. Under 5 free.

Photography, including use of flash, is permitted. There is metered parking on nearby streets and lots.

The ship's location is downtown in Battelle Riverfront Park, at Marconi Blvd. and W. Broad St. Mail: 90 W. Broad St., 1st Floor, Columbus, OH 43215. Phone: 614–645–8760. Fax: 614–645–8748.

Columbus:
Heritage Museum of Kappa Kappa Gamma

Located in University Place, just east of the former Columbus city limits, this mansion was built in 1852–54 by Philip T. Snowden, a dry–goods merchant. The building is designed in the Italianate style, while the woodwork and furnishings reflect tastes of the mid– and late 1800's.

From 1862 to 1864, this mansion was home to Ohio Gov. David Tod. Andrew Johnson, then a Tenn. senator, stayed as a guest of the Governor. From 1865 to 1922 the family of philanthropist David S. Gray lived here. A fire damaged the house and furnishings in 1872, but they were restored.

Today this fine old building serves as a "house museum" and headquarters for the Kappa Kappa Gamma Fraternity. Of special note are the carpeting, draperies, chandeliers, chairs, faux marbled hall, and other interior features.

The Heritage Museum is open year around, Mon.–Fri., 10:00 AM to 4:00 PM, and Sat.–Sun. by appointment. Suggested donations are $2.00 adults and youths 15–18, $1.00 seniors and children under 15.

Photography, including use of flash, is allowed. There's free parking on the street and in a nearby lot.

Address: 530 E. Town St., P.O. Box 38, Columbus, OH 43216. Phone: 614–228–6515. Fax: 614–228–7809.

Columbus:
Kelton House Museum and Garden

An extensive, detailed look into a merchant's house of the late 1800's comes to you in this well-preserved property in central Columbus. Built in 1852 by Fernando and Sophia Kelton, the Greek Revival house contains a large collection of original family possessions, including furniture, garments, decorations, and family records.

Fernando Kelton came to Columbus from Vermont before the Civil War, and joined a wholesale drygoods and pharmaceuticals company owned by John Stone. Kelton was one of 14 honorary pallbearers who accompanied Abraham Lincoln's body through Columbus to the Ohio Statehouse, during the funeral trip from Washington to Springfield, Ill.

Items of particular value and interest in the collection are:

* A grandfather clock by David Burnap, ca. 1790
* Chippendale-style mirrors, ca. 1841
* Brass gaseliers, made 1851-1861
* Staffordshire china cottages, from 1800-1850
* Anna Kelton's scrapbook, providing many insights into the family's history
* A chess table made of paper-mache and inlaid mother-of-pearl, from 1825-1860

The garden shows Victorian influences and the taste of Grace Kelton, a granddaughter of the original occupants. Van Esseltine crabapple trees line the walkway.

A small shop in the museum offers gift items and souvenirs.

The house and garden are open year around on Sun., 1:00 PM to 4:00 PM, and on Mon.-Fri., 10:00 AM to 5:00 PM by appointment. Closed on major U.S. holidays.

Admission is $3.00 adults, $2.00 seniors, $1.50 students 6-18. Children under 6 get in free with an adult.

Photography, including use of flash, is permitted at the discretion of the tour guide. There is parking one block north of the museum on Franklin Ave.

Address: 586 E. Town St., Columbus, OH 43215. Phone: 614-464-2022. Fax: 614-464-3346.

Columbus:
Ohio Craft Museum

This facility has galleries that contain permanent, temporary, and traveling exhibitions of craftware such as baskets, pottery, beads, candles, jewelry, masks, and others. In addition, the museum and its supporting organization, Ohio Designer Craftsmen, conduct workshops, seminars, and demonstrations throughout the year. Children as well as adults can sign up for these. For details, write or call.

The museum is open year around, Mon.-Fri., 10:00 AM to 5:00 PM, and Sun., 1:00 PM to 5:00 PM. Closed Sat. and major national holidays.

Photography, including use of flash, is permitted. There's free parking on an adjacent lot. Admission to the museum is free, but some workshops have a participation fee.

Address: 1665 W. Fifth Ave., Columbus, OH 43212. Phone: 614-486-4402. Fax: 614-486-7110.

Columbus:
Ohio Historical Center

Owned and operated by the Ohio Historical Society, this museum has permanent displays that explore Ohio's history, prehistory, and natural history. Temporary exhibits explain a variety of historical topics, and change year around.

Smaller galleries in the museum feature displays such as the famous "Spirit of '76" painting and the Christopher Collection of interior furnishings and Currier and Ives lithographs.

A large collection of state archives and books is also housed here. The Museum Shop offers books, toys, crafts, replicas, and other gift items relating to Ohio's history.

The Ohio Historical Center is open seven days a week, year around, at various times. Closed on major U.S. holidays. Call or write for details.

Admission fees are $5.00 for adults, seniors, and youths 12-18; and $1.25 for children 6-12. Children under 6 get

72

in free with an adult. The admission fee gives entry to Ohio Village as well as the Museum.

Photography, including use of flash, is permitted. There is ample parking in adjacent lots.

Address: I-71 and 17th Ave., Columbus, OH 43211. Phone: 614-297-2300 or 800-OLD-OHIO.

(Also see Ohio Village next to the Museum.)

Columbus:
Ohio History of Flight Museum

Located on the grounds of Port Columbus Int'l. Airport, this museum features antique aircraft, engines, propellers, and memorabilia of famous Ohio aviators. Highlights include a 1955 Goodyear "Inflate-O-Plane," a replica of a 1914 Wright Model G, a 1961 French SUD Caravelle, and a 1911 Curtiss Model D.

The museum is open year around, seven days a week: Mon.-Fri. 9:00 AM to 4:00 PM, Sat. 12:00 noon to 4:00 PM, and Sun. 1:00 PM to 4:00 PM. Closed on major U.S. holidays.

Photography, including use of flash, is allowed. You'll find free parking in front of the building.

Admission is $3.00 adults, seniors, and youths 16-18, and $2.00 children 4-16. Children under 4 get in free with an adult. In tour-groups of 10 or more, there is $1.00 off the admission price for each person.

Address: 4275 Sawyer Rd., Columbus, OH 43219. Phone: 614-231-1300.

Columbus:
Ohio Village

At this "living historical village," you can experience the daily life of a Civil War-era town. Craftspeople fashion and sell a variety of period items such as baskets, leather goods, and woodblock prints. Other costumed interpreters pursue activities typical of 1860's citizens, including farming, cooking, and playing games.

The Ohio Village Singers and other musicians provide special entertainment on summer weekends and during the Christmas season. Numerous special events, workshops, and reenactments are held throughout the year.

The Village features the Colonel Crawford Inn, a restaurant open for lunch on days when the Village is open. In addition, there's a General Store that sells candy, books, and many other items.

The Ohio Village is open seven days a week, year around, at various times. Closed on major U.S. holidays. Call or write for details.

Admission fees are $5.00 for adults, seniors, and youths 12-18; and $1.25 for children 6-12. Children under 6 get in free with an adult. The admission fee gives you entry to the Ohio Historical Center as well as the Village.

Photography, including use of flash, is permitted. There is ample parking on adjacent lots.

Address: I-77 and 17th Ave., Columbus, OH 43211.
Phone: 614-297-2300 or 800-OLD-OHIO.

(Also see the Ohio Historical Center next to the Village.)

Columbus:
Ohio Women's Hall of Fame

Founded in 1978 by the Ohio Bureau of Employment Services (OBES), this facility provides a public record of contributions made by Ohio women to state, national, and world progress. Members have demonstrated "an extraordinary commitment to excellence, achievement, and service to others," says the brochure.

The Hall of Fame exhibits contain photos and biographies of the most recent inductees, plus the names of all inductees listed by year of induction. A 20-min. videotape explains the Hall of Fame and its history. You can schedule a guided tour by making an appointment.

Located in the OBES building lobby, this facility is open year around, Mon.-Fri., 8:00 AM to 5:00 PM. Closed on weekends and major national holidays. Admission is free.

Photography, including use of flash, is allowed. There's plenty of parking nearby at metered spots on streets and in for–fee lots.

Address: 145 S. Front St., Columbus, OH 43215. Phone: 614–466–4496. Fax: 614–466–7912.

Columbus:
Orton Geological Museum

Located in Orton Hall near the center of The Ohio State University campus, this museum contains more than 500,000 fossil, rock, and mineral specimens. Here you can study many of these, and learn about the science of geology and Ohio's history through geologic time.

Opened in 1893, the building is named after Dr. Edward Orton, Sr. He was OSU's first president, Professor of Geology from 1873 to 1899, and the State Geologist from 1882 to 1899.

The building itself is constructed of 40 different kinds of stone, all native to Ohio. Because of this and other features, Orton Hall has been placed in the National Register of Historic Places.

Outstanding items on display include a skeleton of an Ice Age ground sloth, meteorites of various sizes, and fluorescent minerals. Also exhibited are a full–size replica of a Tyrannosaurus rex skull, teeth from mammoths and mastodons, and a replica of Archaeopteryx, the earliest known bird.

A store in the museum offers models, minerals, fossils, books, posters, and many items relating to dinosaurs.

The museum is open year around, Mon.–Fri., 9:00 AM to 5:00 PM. Tours on weekends can be arranged. Admission is free.

Photography, including use of flash, is permitted. There is parking nearby in the Union Parking Garage (enter on Ramp C). The parking fee begins at $2.00.

Address: Orton Geological Museum, The Ohio State

University, 155 S. Oval Mall, Columbus, OH 43210.
Phone: 614-292-6896. Fax: 614-292-1496.

Columbus:
Thurber House

This three-story brick house was home for two years to
cartoonist and New Yorker writer James Thurber. Features
of the house play roles in stories such as "The Night the
Ghost Got In" and "The Night the Bed Fell." You can see a
typewriter Thurber used while a Columbus Dispatch re-
porter, a room full of first editions, family photos, and
other Thurber memorabilia.

Saved from decay in the early 1980's, Thurber House has
since become something of a literary center. It has a
national writer-in-residence program, two authors' series
for readers, and an annual Thurber birthday party. Writing
classes for children are offered next door in the Thurber
Center.

The Thurber House is open daily year around, 12:00 noon
to 4:00 PM. Guided tours are given on Sun.; on weekdays,
you can take a self-guided tour. Closed on major national
holidays.

Admission is $2.00 for adults taking Sun. tour, $1.50 for
children and seniors. There is free parking and metered on
the street. Photography, including use of flash, is permitted.

Address: 77 Jefferson Ave., Columbus, OH 43215.
Phone: 614-464-1032.

Columbus:
Wexner Center for the Arts

Located on the campus of The Ohio State University, this
facility shows touring exhibitions of contemporary art in
many media. These have included furniture, paintings,
sculpture, architecture, ceramics, glassware, and others.

The Center's bookstore offers gifts and books on
contemporary art, architecture, and film. A cafe in the

Center is open Mon.-Fri., 7:00 AM to 4:00 PM.

Wexner Center galleries are open for viewing year around on Tues., Wed., Fri., and Sat. 10:00 AM to 6:00 PM, Thurs. 10:00 AM to 9:00 PM, and Sun. 12:00 noon to 6:00 PM. Closed on Mon. and major U.S. holidays.

The Center offers walk-in guided tours (no advance registration needed) each Sun. at 1:00 PM. Admission to the galleries is $3.00 adults, $2.00 seniors and visiting students. OSU students, children under 12, and members of the Center get in free. Admission is free on Thurs. and from 5:00 PM to 9:00 PM.

No photography allowed. There is for-pay parking nearby.

Address: The Ohio State Univ., 1871 N. High St., Columbus, OH 43210. Phone: 614-292-3535. Fax: 614-292-3369. Website: www.wexart.org.

Conneaut:
Conneaut Railroad Museum

A former New York Central Railroad depot, built in 1900, is home of this museum. Outside, you can climb into a Bessemer & Lake Erie Railroad caboose, or into a cab of a steam engine donated by the Nickel Plate Railroad. Indoors, features include life-size displays with manikins. They enliven displays of old telegraph equipment, schedule books, photos, and relics pertaining to the Nickel Plate.

The museum contains a large, working, HO-gauge model railroad layout, and exhibits of old stock certificates, photos, timetables, and many other items associated with railroading in the early 1900's.

The museum and outdoor exhibits are open May 1 through Labor Day, seven days a week, 12:00 noon to 5:00 PM. Admission is free; donations help to maintain the facility.

Photography, including use of flash, is allowed. There's free parking next to the museum. A souvenir shop offers a large variety of items.

Address: Depot St., P.O. Box 643, Conneaut, OH 44030. Phone: 440-453-4833.

Directions: From I-90 or SR 20, take SR 7 north into Conneaut to Depot St. The museum is just east of SR 7.

Coshocton:
Roscoe Village

In the early 1800's, Roscoe sprang up on the new Ohio & Erie Canal. One building after another was added, until in 1851 -- the height of canal traffic -- a whole fleet of mule-drawn barges plied the waterway, and the town prospered.

Soon the railroads and highways ate into canal business, however, and Roscoe went into decline. In 1968, Edward and Frances Montgomery, citizens of the area, launched a movement to restore Roscoe to its former glory by turning it into a "living historic village."

Today, most of the old canal bed in the area lies buried under Ohio Route 16. A few blocks north of town, though, you can ride on the horse-drawn "Monticello III," a replica of the first canal barge to stop at Roscoe.

Roscoe Village itself offers many attractions, making it worthwhile to spend an entire day here. Individual buildings include:

* The Toll Collector's House. The original home of Jacob Welsh, Roscoe's first canal tollkeeper, this is now a stop on the "Living History Tour."

* Johnson-Williams House. Built in 1833 by "King" Charley Williams, first white settler in Coshocton County. Later occupied by Dr. Maro Johnson and his family. The house and doctor's office are restored to a mid-1800's look. Don't miss the kitchen downstairs.

* General Store. Has a potbellied stove, old cabinets, and genuine Post Office furnishings from the early 1800's.

* Township Hall. Costumed volunteers demonstrate spinning, weaving, and other crafts from pioneer Roscoe.

* Old Warehouse. Once a storage building for goods being shipped into and out of Roscoe on the canal; now a restaurant.

* Craftsman's House. Using tools, materials, and methods of the early 19th Century, craftsmen turn out woven goods in the old styles.

* Blacksmith Shop. The craft is still practiced here, where many canal mules and horses were shod.

* Johnson–Humrickhouse Museum. Containing extensive exhibits in four galleries on two floors, this museum offers fine displays of prehistoric, Indian, and Early American artifacts; Oriental carvings and porcelain works; and a miscellaneous collection of porcelain, glassware, and carvings from Europe and America.

Also worth a visit is the Triple Lock, a large, deep canal lock that has long been dry. A short drive north of Roscoe, this lock shows the skill of Ohio's early engineers, stone-cutters, and builders.

Roscoe Village is open year around. Numerous special events are held here, including "Dulcimer Days" in May, the "Coshocton Festival" in August, and the "Christmas Candlelightings" in Dec. Write or call for details. Also note that guided tours for clubs, schools, and other groups can be arranged.

The Johnson–Humrickhouse Museum is open Nov. 1–Apr.30, 1:00 PM to 4:30 PM Tues.–Sun. (closed Mon.); also open May 1–Oct. 31, 12:00 noon to 5:00 PM every day. For days and hours of other buildings in the Village, write or call (see below).

From Memorial Day through Labor Day, you can take a ride on the "Monticello III," the replica horse–drawn canal boat. It departs from its dock hourly from 1:00 PM to 5:00 PM daily (from noon to 5:00 PM on July 4 and festival days).

The ride on a restored section of the original Ohio & Erie Canal takes 40 minutes. This attraction is operated by the Coshocton Park District. Fees: $6.00 adults and youths 13–18, $5.00 seniors, $3.00 children 5–12. Younger children get on free with an adult. Special group rates and charter trips are available.

Admission to Roscoe Village is free. Address: Roscoe Village, 381 Hill St., Coshocton, OH 43812. Phone: 614–622–8710.

Photography, including use of flash, is allowed throughout the facility. There's ample free parking in adjacent lots.

Directions: From I-77, take U.S. 36 west to Coshocton. Roscoe is on the western edge of town, at the intersection of U.S. 36 and SR 83.

Crestline:
Crestline Shunk Museum

Housed in the 1860 John Hoffman family residence, this museum collects, preserves, and displays artifacts pertaining to the history of Crestline and the surrounding area. Permanent collections contain historic railroad and Indian artifacts, glassware, china, silverware, toys, and dolls. The house includes a "summer kitchen" and Victorian parlor and bedroom, with turn-of-the-century furniture and decorations.

The museum gets its name from John Q. Shunk, who owned the building until 1953, when he presented it to the Crestline Historical Society. The Society now owns and operates the facility.

Activities include guided tours and lectures.

The museum is open May 1-Sept. 30, on Wed., Sat., and Sun., 2:00 PM to 4:00 PM. Also open at other times by appointment.

Admission: $1.00 adults (18 and up) and seniors, 50 cents children. School classes and tour groups qualify for special group rates.

Photography, including use of flash, is allowed. There's free parking near the building.

Address: 211 N. Thoman St., P.O. Box 456, Crestline, OH 44827. Phone: 419-683-3410.

Dennison:
Dennison Railroad Depot Museum

Located halfway between Pittsburgh and Columbus, Dennison became the site of a huge railroad yard for the Pennsylvania Railroad. During the heyday of passenger rail service -- after the canal era, and before the automobile -- Dennision had some 22 passenger trains stopping every day at its depot.

This 1873 facility became famous nationwide during the early 1940's for its servicemen's canteen. Volunteers from eight counties greeted and fed over 1.5 million servicemen passing through on World War II troop trains.

Now nicely restored, this handsome depot houses a museum, gift shop, and restaurant. Round-trip train excursions depart Dennison on the Ohio Central Railroad for destinations such as Pittsburgh, Zanesville, Newcomerstown, Morgan Run, and Newark. Call or write for details about these excursions.

Displays in the museum show historic photos, railroad and military artifacts, and period depot furnishings. Photography, including use of flash, is allowed. There's free parking next to the depot.

The museum is open year around, Tues.–Sat. 10:00 AM to 5:00 PM, Sun. 11:00 AM to 3:00 PM. Closed on Mon. and major U.S. holidays.

Admission is $3.00 adults, $2.50 seniors, $1.75 students 7–17, and free to those 6 and under.

Address: 400 Center St., P.O. Box 11, Dennison, OH 44621. Phone: 740-922-6776. E-mail: depot@tusco.net. Website: www.dennisondepot.org.

Dover:
Auman Museum of Radio and Television

Housed in two rooms, this collection of early radio and TV sets is said to be "well-known all over the USA," presumably in radio and TV technical circles. See especially the pioneer TV sets built between 1930 and 1950.

Outstanding specimens in the collection include examples of work by radio pioneers Marconi, J.L. Baird, and Bush. The collection also contains samples of some 300 later, U.S.-built models.

The museum is open year around by appointment only. Admission is free. Photography, including use of flash, is allowed. There's free parking on nearby streets.

Address: 4316 Murray Rd. NW, Dover, OH 44622. Phone: 330-364-1058.

(Note: While in Dover, also see Warther's Carvings Museum and the J.E. Reeves Victorian Home.)

Dover:
J.E. Reeves Victorian Home
And Carriage House Museum

In 1900, Jeremiah E. Reeves, a Dover industrialist and banker, remodeled his 19th-Century farmouse and carriage house, and decorated them lavishly in the Victorian style. Now a museum, the two buildings have been carefully re-stored and preserved. The property is owned and operated by the Dover Historical Society, and is on the National Register of Historic Places.

Of special note in the 17-room main house are the orig-inal family furniture, china, and glassware. See also the striking chandeliers, carpeting, wall coverings, and wood-work. A guided tour takes you through all three floors, in-cluding the third-floor ballroom.

In the carriage house, you can see the original Reeves family sleigh and 1892 carriage, a Rauch and Gray electric automobile, a restored doctor's buggy, and a Regina music box. Also on view here are newly developed gardens. There's a gift shop in the carriage house.

This facility is open May 15 through Oct. 31, Tues. through Sun., 10:00 AM to 4:00 PM. Closed on Mon. and major U.S. holidays.

Admission is $5.00 adults, $4.00 seniors, $2.00 students

6-18. Children under 6 get in free with an adult. Special group tours and rates are offered.

The museum staff conducts garden tours June 1 through Sept. 30 on Sat. at 2:00 PM. Also, there is an ice cream social in July, and a style show and tea (by reservation) in Oct. Call or write for more details.

No photography is allowed inside the main house or carriage house. You'll find free parking on nearby streets.

Address: 325 E. Iron Ave. (SR 800 South), Dover, OH 44622. Phone: 330-343-7040 or 800-815-2794.

(P.S.: While in Dover, also see Warther's Carvings Museum and Auman's Museum of Radio and Television.)

Dover:
Warther's Carvings Museum

Ernest "Mooney" Warther, born Oct. 30, 1885, of Swiss immigrant parents, took up carving as a boy. By the time he died in 1973, carving had become a passion, a livelihood, and a source of international fame.

Warther gave away a few carvings, but he refused to sell them. Today you can view them in a 10,000-sq.-ft. museum in Dover, Ohio. The facility includes not only over a hundred carvings, but also a button museum, Warther's original workshop, a knife factory, Swiss floral gardens, and a gift shop. There you can select from dozens of styles of the unique family kitchen knives, plus other types of gifts.

Mooney's father died when the boy was only three years old. At age 14, he went to work in a local steel mill, where he spent 23 years. This inspired his early works, which included a miniature reproduction of the mill, carved from walnut and ivory. On display in the museum, this diorama includes carvings of 17 moveable workmen doing their jobs, a sleeping worker, and an irate foreman.

Warther was always fascinated by railroad trains. This is reflected in the main theme of the museum: the history of steam power and trains, particularly steam locomotives. The museum displays dozens of different types of steam engines, steam locomotives, and complete trains, including:

* Ancient steam engines, such as those designed by Hero, a Greek inventor who lived in Alexandria, Egypt, around 250 BC. Also here: engines by Sir Isaac Newton (Cambridge, 1680), Branca (Rome, 1629), and Leonardo da Vinci (Milan, late 15th C.).

* The "General," famous locomotive of Civil War days, built in 1855.

* The "Commodore Vanderbilt," built at Schenectady in 1870.

* A "Great Northern" mountain-type locomotive, built at the Baldwin Works in 1930.

* The largest ivory carving in the world -- an 8-ft. long, 11,000-piece Empire State Express.

* The Lincoln Funeral Train in ebony, ivory, and pearl.

* A "Hudson" locomotive, designed in 1927 for the New York Central Railroad to pull their "Limited" trains.

Also on display are Mooney's detailed carvings of the "John Bull," our nation's first passenger train, and the famed "Casey Jones" locomotive. An ivory and ebony diorama depicts the driving of the golden spike at Promontory Point, Utah, linking the U.S. East and West by rail.

In all, the museum displays over 11,000 items.

The workshop contains Warther's tools, plus a collection of Indian arrowheads built up over several decades. The button museum holds Mrs. Frieda Warther's collection of some 73,000 buttons. In the knife factory (included in the tour), you can watch Warther's descendents and others fashioning kitchen knives. They're noted for "engine-turning" swirls on the blades.

The 10-acre site also includes an antique steam locomotive and caboose, which you can climb into.

Warther's Carvings Museum is open year around, seven days a week. Hours are: Mar. 1 to Nov. 30, 9:00 AM to 5:00 PM; Dec. 1 to Feb. 28, 10:00 AM to 4:00 PM. Closed on Easter, Thanksgiving, Christmas, and New Year's Day.

Admission: $7.00 adults (incl. seniors), $3.00 students 7-17. Children under 6 get in free with an adult.

Your admission fee includes a guided tour lasting about 1 hr. Special group rates and tours can be arranged. Photography, including use of flash, is allowed. There's free parking on the museum grounds.

Address: 331 Karl Ave., Dover, OH 44622. Phone: 330-343-7513. Fax: 330-364-4228.

Directions: From I-77, get off at Exit 83, the Dover-Sugar Creek exit (SR 39). Go 1/4-mile east on SR 39, then angle right (southeast) on SR 211 (Tuscarawas Ave.). Go one block. The museum is on the right-hand (southwest) side.

East Liverpool:
Museum of Ceramics

From about 1850 to the mid-1930's, East Liverpool, Ohio, was the nation's leading producer of household ceramics or "crockery." In fact, the city acquired the nickname "America's Crockery City."

This pre-eminence in the industry was made possible by the city's location on the Ohio River (good for transportation), and by the abundance of clay and coal deposits nearby. Also contributing were the influx of entrepreneurs, skilled artisans from England, and ample labor from Ireland and other countries.

The first of the entrepreneurs was English-born James Bennett. Along with his brother and other skilled potters, he founded the town's first pottery business in 1839. Other businessmen and artisans who built up the local industry included Benjamin Harker, William Brunt, Jabez Vodrey, Thomas Croxall, William Bloor, and John Goodwin.

By 1900, over 90 percent of the city's workers were somehow connected with the ceramic industry. Today that period is commemorated in East Liverpool's 11,000-sq.-ft. Museum of Ceramics. Administered by the Ohio Historical Society, Columbus, the museum occupies the former City Post Office, built in 1909. The building is noted for its ornate interior trim, including floors of marble and terrazo.

Displays include an extensive array of wares made by local potteries in their heyday, as well as dioramas showing how pottery was made. Among the museum's prized possessions is a collection of Lotus Ware, made by Knowles, Taylor, and Knowles between 1891 and 1897. Lotus Ware is famous for its pure white color, lustrous finish, graceful shapes, and fine detailing.

The museum is open Mar. 1–Nov. 30, Wed. through Sun. Hours are 9:30 AM to 5:00 PM Wed.–Sat., and 12:00 noon to 5:00 PM Sun. Closed on Mon. and Tues.

Fees are: $5.00 adults, $4.50 seniors, $1.25 children 6–12. Younger children get in free with an adult. Guided tours are available.

There's free parking in a lot behind the museum and on nearby streets. Photography, including use of flash, is permitted.

The museum holds special events throughout its nine-month season. You can view a nine-projector sound and slide show on the city's history and its ceramics industry. A gift shop offers publications and memorabilia.

For more details, write to: Museum of Ceramics, 400 E. Fifth St., East Liverpool, OH 43920. Phone: 330–386–6001. Fax: 330–386–0488.

Eastlake:
Croatian Heritage Museum

One of several ethnic-heritage museums in Northeast Ohio, this one displays collections of Croatian artifacts, textiles, folk costumes, wood carvings, sculpture, metalwork, leather objects, lacework, and paintings. A library in the building contains 13,500 volumes of books and periodicals in Croatian and English.

The museum holds special events at Christmans and Easter. Guided tours are offered.

Open year around on Fri., 7:00 PM to 10:00 PM or by appointment at other times. Admission is free; donations welcome.

Photography, including use of flash, is allowed. There's free parking on the museum grounds.

Address: 34900 Lakeshore Blvd., Eastlake, OH 44095. Phone: 330-386-6001. Fax: 330-386-0488.

Elyria:
The Hickories Museum

Named after the many shag-bark hickory trees on the one-acre grounds surrounding it, this 1890's mansion was the home of Arthur L. Garford, a local industrialist. The 32-room, three-story residence contains Tiffany-style windows, six fireplaces, 16 built-in seats, and about 60 carved faces. The woodwork in many of the rooms is done in cherry, Mexican mahogany, or English oak.

Features of the main staircase are pier mirrors, a Gothic chapel, and a stuffed bull-moose head. The head was given to Mr. Garford by Pres. Teddy Roosevelt in appreciation for financial support to the Bullmoose Party.

The museum is owned and operated by the Lorain County Historical Society, which has offices in the building. The Hick's Memorial Library occupies space on the second floor.

The Hickories Museum is open Mar. 1 through Nov. 30. The staff offers guided tours Tues. through Fri. at 1:00, 2:00, and 3:00 PM, or by appointment at other times. Closed Dec. 1-Feb. 28; on Mon., Sat., and Sun.; and on major U.S. holidays.

Admission: $3.50 ages 12 and up, $1.00 children under 12. Discounts are offered for groups of 10 or more.

No photography is allowed inside the museum. You'll find free parking on a lot behind the building and on nearby streets.

Address: 509 Washington Ave., Elyria, OH 44035. Phone: 440-322-3341.

Euclid:
Cleveland Hungarian Heritage Museum

It's been said that Cleveland is home to more Hungarians than any city except Budapest. Serving their cultural and archival needs is the Cleveland Hungarian Heritage Society. Founded in 1985, the society operates a new museum in Euclid Square Mall, Euclid.

This facility, opened in May, 1999, displays traditional Hungarian folk costumes, ceramics, and other artifacts. Rare photos tell of Cleveland's Hungarian neighborhoods, which began forming in the 1880's. A gift shop offers books, mementoes, and artifacts for sale.

The CHHM is open year around on Wed. 2:00 PM to 8:00 PM; on Thurs. and Sat. 11:00 AM to 5:00 PM; and by request for special occasions. Closed on major U.S. holidays.

Admission is free. You may take snapshots in the museum. There's ample free parking in the mall lot.

Address: 300 Euclid Square Mall, Euclid, OH 44132. Phone: 216-289-9400. Fax: 440-442-3466.

Euclid:
Euclid Hist. Soc. Museum

Housed in what once was Euclid Township's first high school, this museum collects, preserves, and displays arti-facts, photos, maps, documents, and other items that il-luminate Euclid's past. The property is owned and admin-istered by the Euclid Historical Society, founded in 1958.

Among the displays are:

* Furnished rooms showing examples of living, sleeping, and children's play areas in the Victorian Era

* A furnished kitchen from the 1800's, including utensils

* A collection of carpenter's tools from the turn of the century

* Examples of arc lights and other inventions by Charles F. Brush, a Euclid native who developed and introduced street illumination in Cleveland

* Examples of duplicating and address-plate manufacturing equipment from the former Addressograph-Multigraph Corp.

The museum is open on every Tues. and on the last Sun. of every month, from 1:00 PM to 4:00 PM. Tours at other times can be arranged by appointment.

Admission is free. Photography, including use of flash, is permitted. You'll find free parking on a city lot on North St., behind the Baptist Bible Temple.

Address: 21129 North St., Euclid, OH 44117. Phone: 216-289-8577.

Directions: From Euclid Ave., go north on Chardon Rd. one block to North St., and turn east (right). The museum is on the north (left) side.

Euclid:
National Cleveland-Style
Polka Hall of Fame

Sponsored by the American-Slovenian Polka Foundation, this facility preserves and promotes Cleveland-style polka music. The style comes from Slovenian origins, and is influenced by American popular music. Soon after World War II, Cleveland became widely known as a major polka center, thanks largely to this music style.

The Hall of Fame has inductions each year. Displays in the facility depict the history of Cleveland-style polka music. A well-stocked store in the building sells cassettes and CDs featuring many popular and famous polka bands.

The Hall of Fame is open year around on Mon., Thurs., and Fri. 12:00 noon to 5:00 PM; Tues. 3:00 PM to 7:00 PM; and Sat. 11:00 AM to 2:00 PM. Closed on Wed., Sun., and major U.S. holidays.

Admission is free. Photography, including use of flash, is allowed. There's free parking in the front and back of the building.

Address: Shore Cultural Center, 291 E. 222nd St., Euclid, OH 44123. Phone: 216-261-3263. Fax: Same.

Fairport Harbor:
Fairport Marine Museum

Founded in 1945 by the Fairport Harbor Historical Society, this is the first lighthouse marine museum in the U.S. It supports and perpetuates marine traditions of the area and the Great Lakes.

The tower, built originally in 1825, was rebuilt in 1871 of gray sandstone. It stands 60 ft. tall, and contains a spiral staircase of 69 steps leading to an observation platform. The tower was decommissioned and replaced in 1925.

In the lightkeeper's house next to the tower, a museum displays ship models, an old lighthouse lens, Indian relics, and old maps and pioneer documents pertaining to Fairport and the Grand River. Also on display are ship navigation instruments, marine paintings, ship carpenter's tools, ore samples, and other artifacts.

Next to the museum is a reconstructed ship's pilothouse taken from the former Great Lakes ore carrier "Frontenac." The pilothouse includes the types of wheel, instruments, and other appointments typical of older ore carriers.

The museum, tower, and pilothouse are open on Wed., Sun., and holidays, 1:00 PM to 6:00 PM, from Memorial Day weekend through the second weekend in Sept. Admission is $2.00 adults, $1.00 seniors and children.

Photography is allowed, but no flash. There's free parking on nearby streets. Tours by school classes and other groups are welcome, by appointment.

Address: 129 Second St., Fairport Harbor, OH 44077. Phone: 440-354-4825.

Directions: From I-90 or U.S. 20, take SR 44 north to SR 535. Take 535 north to Fairport Rd., which forks to the left. Follow Fairport Rd. north to High St., which forks to the right. The museum is at High and Second Sts.

Garfield Heights:
Garfield Heights Historical Museum

Also known as "The Teachers' House," this 1890 residence served for 63 years as home for teachers at the St. John Evangelical Lutheran Church. Five different teachers and their families occupied it between 1890 and 1953.

In 1955, a new owner -- Mr. Joseph Ellis -- bought the home and moved it to its present location on Turney Rd. The house became a museum in 1992. It is operated by the Garfield Heights Historical Society, which has offices in the building. The City of Garfield Heights owns the home.

Attractions here include:

* Garfield Heights Room. Historical photos and a library.

* Military and Radio Room. Uniforms, military radios, other items.

* Kitchen. See a 1930's stove and refrigerator, plus utensils, dishes, and glassware.

* Vern Lewis Room. Books, historical photos, old magazines and newspapers. May be used for historical research.

* Rose Weed Room. Collections of clothing, bedding, toys, dolls, antique chairs, sewing machines, and an antique dresser and bed.

* Utility Room. On display are a 1950's amateur radio station, crystal radio set, and an old teletype machine. Also, collections of pots, pans, irons, bottles, ice skates, roller skates, sleds, tools, and a weaving loom.

* TV Room. Collections of early clocks, table radios, typewriters, pipes, cameras, Indian artifacts, and spinning wheels. Also, audio and video cassette tapes of historical interest.

The museum is open year around on Sat. 1:00 PM to 4:00 PM, or by appointment. There's no admission charge. Photography, including use of flash, is permitted. You'll find free parking at the side of the home.

Address: 5405 Turney Rd., Garfield Heights, OH 44125. Phone: 216-587-3369.

Geneva:
Shandy Hall Museum

Considered a mansion when built in 1815, Shandy Hall contains 17 rooms, including the original cellar kitchen, with cooking fireplace, bake oven, and buttery. The formal parlor features American Empire furniture, while the banquet room has a coved ceiling and scenic 1815 French wallpaper.

Administered by the Western Reserve Historical Society, Cleveland, Shandy Hall is a well-preserved example of grand living in the early 19th Century. The mansion is open May 1 to Oct. 31, six days a week. Hours are: Tues.-Sat. 10:00 AM to 5:00 PM, Sun. 12:00 noon to 5:00 PM. Closed Mon.

Admission: $3.00 for adults, $2.00 for seniors and children. Group rates and special tours are available. There is free parking on the site. Management allows photography, but no use of flash.

For more details, write to: Shandy Hall, 6333 S. Ridge Road West, Geneva, OH 44041. Tel.: 440-466-3680.

Directions: From I-90, go north on Rte. 528 to Madison. Turn east (right) on Rte. 84, go 3.6 miles. Shandy Hall is one mile east of Unionville on 84.

Gnadenhutten:
Gnadenhutten Historical Park

In Oct., 1772, Joshua -- a Mohican Indian who had been converted to a Moravian Christian sect -- brought a large group of fellow converted Mohicans from Pennsylvania to this location about 11 miles south of New Philadelphia. The settlement prospered, and soon there were 50 to 60 log buildings here.

Their standard of living was high for frontier Ohio. The Christian Mohicans had glass windows in their cabins, used pewter utensils, and were adept at crafts and artwork.

Then, in 1781, British troops and their Indian allies surrounded the settlement, took the Mohicans captive, and moved them to a distant town. Conditions got so bad in captivity, however, that the Mohicans asked and got permission to return to Gnadenhutten and bring back whatever food they could carry. While in their settlement, the Mohicans -- taken for British allies -- were rounded up and slaughtered by Pennsylvania militiamen. Two boys escaped and told the story.

Seventeen years later, Moravian missionary John Heckleweller returned, buried the Mohicans' bones, and began a second Christian village. This was a white settlement, which has evolved into the present town of Gnadenhutten (pop. 1,226). It is regarded as the oldest continuous settlement in Ohio.

Today the five-acre Gnadenhutten Historical Park honors those early Mohican and white settlers. The Park contains a monument, gravesite, reconstructed cabins, and a museum. In it, you can view household items used in early Gnadenhutten, along with the settlers' books, Bibles, and journals.

The staff holds special events throughout the open season. This goes from June 1 to Aug. 31, Mon.-Sat., 10:00 AM to 5:00 PM, and Sun. 12:00 noon to 5:00 PM. In addition, you can visit from Sept. 1 to Oct. 31, on Sat. 10:00 AM to 5:00 PM, and Sun. 12:00 noon to 5:00 PM. The Park is open at any time by appointment.

Admission is free; donations welcome. No photography permitted. There's free parking on the site.

Address: P.O. Box 396, Gnadenhutten, OH 44629. Phone: 740-254-4143. Fax: 740-254-4986. Location: Ten miles east of I-77 on SR36.

(Gnadenhutten means "Huts of Grace" in the Moravian German dialect. It is pronounced Ja-na-den-hut-en.)

SECTION 4 -- GRANVILLE THROUGH MENTOR

Granville:
Granville Historical Museum

Housed in an 1816 bank building, this museum commemorates the history of Granville and the surrounding area.
Collections include pre-1850 carpenter tools, and items
relating to local geology, military history, textiles, costumes,
and decorative arts. Some items date back to 1805. The
Granville Historical Society administers the museum.

Open Apr. 1-Oct. 31, Sat. and Sun., 1:00 PM to 4:00
PM, and at other times by appointment. Admission is free;
donations welcome.

Photography, including use of flash, is permitted. There's
limited free parking on nearby streets.

Address: 115 E. Broadway, P.O. Box 129, Granville,
OH 43023. Phone: 740-587-3951.

Granville:
Granville Lifestyle Museum

The H.D. Robinson House, built in 1870-71, has been
preserved in the style of Hubert and Oese Robinson, who
died in 1960 and 1981, respectively. On display are furnishings and family possessions from four generations. Of
particular interest:

* A Steinway piano built in 1911. Visitors are invited to
play it.

* Original walnut woodwork with oak trim

* A 1940 crystal chandelier

* Reproduction photo of Edgar Allan Poe, taken by
Marcus A. Root, born in Granville

* Late Victorian bedroom furniture

* 1949 kitchen with banquette

* Family photos (1890-1970's) exhibited with the
objects in the photos

94

Listed on the National Register of Historic Places, the house is open from mid–Apr. to mid–Oct., Sun. only, 1:00 PM to 4:00 PM, and at other times by appointment. Guided group tours with a program can be arranged for Mon.–Sat.

Admission is $2.00 on Sun.; children under 12 get in free with an adult. No photography allowed. There's free parking in front and on nearby streets.

Address: 121 S. Main St., P.O. Box 134, Granville, OH 43023. Phone: 740-587-0373.

(P.S.: While in Granville, also see the Robbins–Hunter Museum, Granville Historical Museum, and Granville Historic District.)

Granville:
Robbins Hunter Museum

This museum is part of Granville's Historic District. Located about 25 miles east of Columbus, Granville was settled in 1805 by 170 people in 26 families from Granville, Mass., and five nearby towns. The settlers came to take advantage of Ohio's fertile land, because their poor New England soil could not produce enough to support the growing local population.

In 1816, the Granville Furnace began making cast–iron tools and parts for wagons. The following year, a tannery began turning out leather for saddles, harnesses, and shoes, and by 1825 a clock factory went into production. Soon thereafter, an Ohio & Erie feeder canal came to the south end of Main St., beginning several decades of prosperity for Granville.

Today 67 buildings in the center of town are on the National Register of Historic Places. A self–guided walking tour (map provided) takes you past 35 of the 67, and optionally into several. Buildings open for visits include:

* The Avery Downer House, now the Robbins Hunter Museum. Built in the Greek Revival style in 1842 for Alfred Avery, a local merchant. Open year around as a museum of the Licking County Historical Society. Head-

quarters and starting point for tours of the Historic Village area.

* The Mower–Heisey House. A fine example of the Federal style championed by Thomas Jefferson and others. Lucius Mower was an early businessman in the area. This is now a private residence.

* The Granville Inn. Modeled after a 16th Century Tudor manor house, it was built of stone and timber in 1924.

* The Buxton Inn. Built orginally in 1812 by Orrin Granger; remodelled extensively in 1820 and 1850. A Major Horton Buxton bought it in 1865, and operated it as an inn until 1902. It is now Ohio's oldest continuously operating inn that uses the original building.

Your tour begins at the Robbins Hunter Museum, which includes an extensive collection of decorative objects from the 1800's. Open May 1–Nov. 30, Tues. through Sun., 1:00 PM to 4:00 PM. Closed on Mon. and Dec. 1–Apr. 30.

Admission is $2.00 a person. There's free parking on the street in front of the museum and nearby. No photography allowed inside the museum or other buildings.

Address: 221 E. Broadway, P.O. Box 183, Granville, OH 43023. Phone: 740–587–0430.

Hiram:
John Johnson Farm House

Built in 1829, this house was home to farmer John Johnson and his wife Elsa. In 1831, the Johnsons invited Joseph Smith, Jr. –– prophet and leader of the Church of Jesus Christ of Latter Day Saints (Mormons) –– to live with them. Smith, his wife Emma, and their adopted twins moved in.

One night in March, 1832, a mob dragged Smith from his bed to a nearby field, beat him, and tarred and feathered him. He bore scars from that event for the rest of this life.

Today the farm produces apples and strawberries. Harvested fruit is shipped to welfare facilities that feed the poor and needy. The house itself is operated as a visitors' center and museum, which contains period furniture, tools, etc., in the kitchen and bedrooms.

Admission is free. The staff conducts guided tours daily from 9:00 AM to dusk. To make reservations or schedule a group tour, call 330-569-3170. (Closed as of this writing, the home will reopen in the summer of 2000.)

There's free parking on the premises. No snapshots, please.

Address: 6203 Pioneer Trail Rd., Hiram, OH 44234.

Directions: From the junction of SRs 44 and 82 in Mantua Corners, drive east on 82 about 1.5 miles to Vaughan Rd. Turn south, go 0.5 mile to Pioneer Trail Rd. Turn east, go 2.0 miles to the farm.

Jefferson:
Jefferson Depot Railroad Museum

On June 10, 1863, stockholders of the Cleveland, Painesville, and Ashtabula Railroad Co. agreed to extend the line through Ashtabula County. This would connect the line with the railroad's Jamestown and Franklin Division at the Pa. state line. By 1879, the extension of the Lake Shore and Michigan Southern Railroad to Jefferson brought the town's station a total of 14,635 passengers a year. By 1902, some 15 passenger trains stopped at Jefferson every day.

Most county residents came by train (there were no autos yet) to pay their taxes, as Jefferson was the county seat. One of the first sidewalks in town ran from the depot to the county courthouse to accommodate taxpayers.

Today the restored, 120-ft.-long depot is open on Sun. for touring during June, July, and Aug. Hours are 1:00 PM to 4:00 PM. Admission is $2.00 for adults and seniors; people 18 and under get in free.

Your tour may include not only the depot but also a 1918 Pennsylvania Railroad caboose, a Century barn, 1848 church, and 1838 one-room schoolhouse. Group tours are available on request.

You'll find free parking on the grounds. Photography, including use of flash, is permitted.

Listed on the National Register of Historic Places, Jefferson Depot is at 147 E. Jefferson St., P.O. Box 22, Jefferson, OH 44047. Phone: 440-293-5532 or 440-576-6305.

Jefferson:
Victorian Perambulator Museum

It's a convenience, often a necessity, and -- if old, rare, and beautiful -- a collectible. The perambulator, also called the baby buggy or carriage, holds center stage at this 4,000-sq.-ft. museum in Jefferson, Ohio.

Founded in 1988 by sisters Judith Kaminski and Janet Pallo, the privately owned facility has nine rooms filled with antique baby and doll perambulators, dolls, doll clothing, photos, books, and toys. As far as the owners can determine, this is the only museum of its kind in the world.

Among the rare specimens on display are an 1885 F.A. Whitney carriage, a French puppet stage, an 1880s Gondola carriage, a French "Bebe Jumeau" doll, and a 34" Simon Halbig doll. Also shown are a high-wheel Huffy bicycle from the early 1900s, an 1870s Wakefield rattan twin carriage, and a 200-year-old high chair.

The museum is open Sept. 1 to May 31 on Sat., and June 1 to Aug. 31 on Wed. and Sat. Hours on these days is 11:00 AM to 5:00 PM. Tours on other days can be arranged by appointment.

Admission: $3.00 adults, $2.50 children. No photography allowed. Special group rates are offered. There's a museum store on the premises. Parking is free.

The address: 26 E. Cedar St., Jefferson, OH 44047. Phone: 440-576-9588.

Directions: From I-90, exit south on Rte. 46. Go about five miles south to Jefferson; turn left (east) on Cedar.

Kent:
Kent State University Museum

Located on the university campus, this museum has nine galleries featuring changing exhibitions by many of the world's top artists and designers. With emphasis on fashion and decorative arts, most of the world's major cultures are represented. The museum also houses a significant collection of American glass. Recent exhibitions have featured glass-work from Ohio, Pennsylvania, and West Virginia; paintings from India; and Chinese ivory carvings.

The museum is open year around on Wed., Fri., and Sat. 10:00 AM to 4:45 PM; Thurs. 10:00 AM to 8:45 PM; and Sun. 12:00 noon to 4:45 PM. Closed on Mon., Tues., and major U.S. holidays.

Admission: $5.00 adults, $4.00 seniors, $3.00 students 7-18. Children 6 and under get in free with an adult.

No photography allowed. There's plenty of free parking nearby.

Address: Rockwell Hall, KSU, P.O. Box 5190, Kent, OH 44242. Phone: 330-
72-3450. Fax: 330-672-3218. Website: www.kent.edu/museum.

Kidron:
Kidron Community Hist. Soc. Museum

Located across the street from Lehman's Hardware, this building includes a museum, gift shop, and Department of Genealogy. The last-named includes computer databases containing over one million names of Amish, Swiss Men-nonite, and German Mennonite families. Some family lines can be traced back to the 1500's in Europe.

The museum tells the story of Swiss Mennonite immigrants who settled this area, beginning in 1819. In addition, there are displays of locally handmade wooden cabinets, tables, chairs, benches, boxes, and barrels. Other types of artifacts on display are shoes, books, dolls, toys, mats, and paintings, plus a working loom and woven goods.

Special events are held nearby throughout the year. Write for details about livestock auctions, flea markets, barbeques, machinery sales, and others.

You can tour the Center June 1–Sept. 30 on Tues., Thurs., and Sat., 11:00 AM to 3:00 PM; also Oct. 1–May 30 on Thurs. and Sat., 11:00 AM to 3:00 PM. Closed on Sun., Mon., and major U.S. holidays. Group tours can be arranged.

Admission is free, but the Center requests donations of $4.00 adults and seniors, $2.00 students 6–18. Children under 6 get in free with an adult.

Photos may be taken with permission of the host. (Do not photograph the Amish.) There is free parking next to the building.

Address: 13153 Emerson Rd. (County Rd. 80), P.O. Box 234, Kidron, OH 44636. Phone: 330–857–9111.

Directions: This museum is at the intersection of County Roads 52 and 80 in the center of Kidron. There's easy access from the south, west, and north.

Kirtland:
Kirtland Temple Historic Center

This church, dedicated in 1836, was erected by members of the Church of Latter Day Saints, also known as the Mormons, and is now owned by the Reorganized Church of the Latter Day Saints. It was the first house of worship for followers of Joseph Smith, Jr., who founded the movement in New York State in the early 1830's.

Built of local sandstone and timber, the entire structure is now a "church museum." It is listed as a National Historic Landmark.

The pulpits and pews are among outstanding features of the interior. Each of the two floors has two pulpits, one at the front and one at the back, for a total of four pulpits. On the main floor, benches in the pew boxes can be turned around. This makes it possible to have the congregation face either a front or rear pulpit.

The Temple is open for touring by the public year around, Mon.-Sat. 9:00 AM to 5:00 PM, and Sun. 1:00 PM to 5:00 PM. Closed on major U.S. and Christian holidays. Admission is free.

No photography allowed indoors. There is free parking next to the building.

Address: 9020 Chillicothe Rd., Kirtland, OH 44094. Phone: 440-256-3318.

Kirtland:
N.K. Whitney Store Museum

Owned by N.K. Whitney, this building was used as a country store. Displays show early fabrics, firearms, bullets, an 1836 store ledger, and other artifacts. The Whitney home across the street serves as a visitor center.

Admission is free. You may visit the store any day, year around. Months and hours are: Apr. 1–Sept. 30, 9:00 AM to 7:00 PM; and Oct 1–Mar. 31, 9:00 AM to 5:00 PM. Closed on Thanksgiving and Christmas.

There's free parking next to the building. Photography, including use of flash, is permitted.

Address: 8876 Chillicothe Rd., SR 306, Kirtland, OH 44094. Phone: 440-256-9805.

Lakeside:
Heritage Hall Museum

Lakeside is a gated, Victorian summer resort on Lake Erie, with a nominal, two-hour gate fee during the season. Called "The Chautauqua of the Great Lakes" by some, the facility has a small museum that displays not only resort memorabilia, but also relics from the Johnson's Island prison camp. In that Civil War facility, the Union Army held Confederate officers.

Administered by the Lakeside Heritage Society, the museum is open June 1 through Labor Day, Tues.-Sat., 9:00

AM to 12:00 PM and 1:00 PM to 4:00 PM; also on Sun. 1:30 PM to 4:30 PM. Closed on Mon. and major U.S. holidays.

No photography permitted. There's ample free parking on the grounds. Admission is free; donations accepted.

Address: Heritage Hall Museum, 238 Maple Ave., Lakeside, OH 43440. Phone: 419-798-5519.

Directions: Lakeside is just west of Sandusky, on the north edge of the Marblehead Peninsula.

Lakewood:
Oldest Stone House Museum

This house was built in 1838 by John Honam, a weaver from Scotland, using sandstone quarried nearby. The house served as a residence for various tenants until 1870, then became at different times a post office, shoe-repair shop, grocery store, doctor's office, upholsterer's store, and barbershop.

In 1952, the Lakewood Historical Society had the building moved to it present site. They then furnished it with period pieces, gathered historical artificts, and opened the house as a museum in 1954. On display are furniture, spinning wheels, household items, clothing, tools, toys, books, and dolls -- all from Lakewood's early days.

You can tour a large kitchen, furnished parlor, and two upstairs bedrooms. Behind the house is an herb garden.

Linked to this stone house as a sister facility is the Nicholson House, a frame building built in 1835. Here the parlors are restored to the mid-Victorian period. James Nicholson (b. 1782, d. 1859), Lakewood's first permanent resident on Detroit Ave., organized the town's first church and helped to build the area's first schoolhouse.

Both houses are listed in the National Register of Historic Places.

Special services provided by the Museum include periodic demonstrations of spinning and quilting, slide presentations on Lakewood history, talks for school children, and others. Call or write for details.

The Nicholson House can be rented for meetings, lunch-eons, and other occasions.

Tours of the Oldest Stone House Museum are conducted by costumed hostesses on Wed. 1:00 PM to 4:00 PM, and Sun. 2:00 PM to 5:00 PM, Feb. 1 through Nov. 30. Closed in Dec. and Jan., and on major U.S. holidays. Visits by school classes, clubs, and other groups can be arranged.

Admission is free; donations are welcome. There's free parking near the museum. Photography is not permitted inside.

Address: 14710 Lake Ave., Lakewood, OH 44107. Phone: 216-221-7343.

Lexington:
Richland County Museum

This museum collects, preserves, and displays objects that reveal the history of Lexington and Richland County. There are permanent exhibits of historic farm implements, Indian artifacts, old medical equipment, and fine needlework from the 1800's. The staff offers guided tours for individuals, families, and groups.

The museum is open May 1 through Sept. 30, Sat. and Sun., 1:30 PM to 4:30 PM. Closed on major U.S. holidays.

Admission is free; donations welcome. Photography, in-cluding use of flash, is allowed. You'll find free parking in front of the museum and on nearby streets.

Address: 51 Church St., P.O. Box 3154, Lexington, OH 44904. Phone: 419-884-2230.

Lisbon:
Lisbon Historic District

There are now 60 homes and other buildings on the Ohio Historic Inventory in the Village of Lisbon, about 22 miles south of Youngstown. A section of Lisbon has been des-ignated a Historic District because of its early history and architecture. The second-oldest town in Ohio, Lisbon boasts nearly all the early American architectural styles.

Among the buildings open for viewing are the Old Stone House Museum at 100 E. Washington St., and the Erie Railroad Station, also on this street. Built in 1803–05, the house is thought to be the oldest standing stone residence in Ohio. Erected by town founder Lewis Kinney, it was originally a tavern and meeting house. It contains many furnishings and memorabilia from the early 1800's.

The Erie Railroad Station was a combination passenger station, freight station, and freight warehouse. The railroad came to Lisbon in 1865.

Many other buildings in the Historic District are open to the public, but are now privately owned. The Lisbon Historical Society will provide a map for a walking tour.

Six miles west of Lisbon is Fort Tuscaroras, with memorabilia from the Revolution, War of 1812, and Civil War. Also, about four miles west of Lisbon is the Rebecca Furnace. Built in 1808, it was one of the first charcoal iron furnaces in Ohio. The operator was James McKinley, grandfather of Pres. Wm. McKinley. Museum staff members can direct you to these sites.

Admission to the two museums costs $1.00 a person. For days and times the museums are open, call 330–424–9000 or 330–424–1861. Photography, including use of flash, is permitted in the museums. There's free parking on the streets.

Address: Lisbon Historical Society, 117/119 E. Washington St., P.O. Box 191, Lisbon, OH 44432. Phone: 330–424–5905.

Lorain:
Moore House Museum

Built in 1906 by a local businessman and civic leader, the Moore House is filled with items from early Lorain. These include furniture, photos, kitchen utensils, toys, and many others. On file here are articles and photos detailing Lorain's history.

Headquarters of the Black River Historical Society, the Museum is open year around, Wed. and Sun., 1:00 PM to 4:00 PM. You can arrange for group tours anytime with prior reservations.

Admission: $2.00 adults and seniors, $1.00 students under 18. Children under 6 get in free with an adult. Photography is permitted, but no flash. There's free parking next to the building.

Address: 309 Fifth St., Lorain, OH 44052. Phone: 440-245-2563.

Loudonville:
Cleo Redd Fisher Museum

Dedicated in 1974, this museum commemorates events and people who helped shape the town of Loudonville. The museum was built with funds donated by the late Mrs. Fisher, a lifelong resident. The Mohican Historical Society administers the facility.

On display are collections of Victorian furniture, muzzle-loading rifles (all made in Loudonville), Indian artifacts found in the area, old tools, and medical instruments. An animated village exhibit "is always a big hit with young and old," according to the director.

Other exhibits honor individuals who lived in the area and made significant contributions to Loudonville or the country as a whole. Among them is the inventor Charles F. Kettering, a native son.

The museum is open from Memorial Day through Labor Day, on Sat., Sun., and holidays, 2:00 PM to 5:00 PM. Tours can be scheduled for any day by calling 419-994-5800 or 419-994-4050.

Admission is 50 cents for adults, seniors, and youths 12-18; 25 cents for children 6-12. Children under 6 get in free with an adult.

Photography, including use of flash, is permitted. There is limited free parking on nearby streets.

Address: 203 E. Main St., Loudonville, OH 44842. Phone: 419-994-4050.

Lucas:
Malabar Farm

Once the estate of Pulitzer prize-winning author Louis Bromfield, Malabar Farm -- now an Ohio State Park -- contains the author's 32-room mansion called "Big House." Bromfield wrote a dozen screenplays for Hollywood, and among his friends who visited Malabar were many celebrities. In 1945, Humphrey Bogart and Lauren Bacall were married here.

Besides writing novels and screenplays, Bromfield was a dedicated, inventive agronomist. He pioneered techniques for lessening soil erosion and building more fertile soil. Taken for granted today, these techniques were as simple as contour plowing, crop rotation, and fertilizing with manure.

You can tour the Big House, farm buildings, and nearby grounds. A highlight in the mansion is a pair of valuable Grandma Moses paintings. Special events are held each month throughout the year. They include the annual "Ohio Heritage Days" in Sept. and "Christmas at Malabar" in Dec.

Photography is permitted throughout the park and in the Big House, but no flash, please. There's ample free parking on two lots.

Fees for admission to the grounds (building tours included) are: $3.00 adults, $2.70 seniors, $1.00 children 6-17. Children under 6 get in free with an adult.

You can take a tractor-drawn tour of the farm during the summmer months. Fees are $1.00 for adults, $.90 for seniors and children 6-18. Children under 6 ride free.

The park is open year around; days and hours vary with the seasons. Write or call for details.

Address: Malabar Farm, 4050 Bromfield Rd., Lucas, OH 44843. Phone: 419-892-2784. Fax: 419-892-3988. Website: www.malabarfarm.org.

Directions: From I-71, get off at Exit 169, heading southeast toward Bellville. Take Hanley Rd. east to Little Washington Rd. (2 miles), and turn right (south). When you reach Pleasant Valley Rd., bear left. Follow this road 7 miles to Bromfield Rd. Turn right into the park.

Mansfield:
Kingwood Center

Originally the estate of Ohio industrialist Charles K. King, this restored and well-preserved center on 47 acres includes display gardens and a Norman French chateau. Built in 1926, the 20,000-sq.-ft. mansion has 11 major rooms, 10 smaller rooms, 10 bathrooms, and 12 fireplaces.

Included on the grounds are a horticultural library and greenhouse. The gardens offer seasonal showings of daffodils, tulips, wildflowers, irises, peonies, roses, daylilies, and others flowers.

Since 1976, the estate has been on the National Register of Historic Places.

The gardens and greenhouse are open daily year around. The chateau, called Kingwood Hall, is open Tues.-Sat. in winter, Tues.-Sun. in summer. Closed on Thanksgiving, Christmas, and New Year's Day. Hours vary according to season; write or call for details.

Admission is free. You may take snapshots in Kingwood Hall (no tripods inside), in the outbuildings, and on the grounds. There is free parking on nearby lots and on Linden Rd.

Address: 900 Park Ave. West, Mansfield, OH 44906. Phone: 419-522-0211.

Directions: From I-71, exit at U.S. 30 West. Drive west to SR 42; turn south to Park Ave. The estate is near the intersection of Park Ave. and Trimble Rd., on Mansfield's west side.

Mansfield:
Oak Hill Cottage

Built in 1847, this fine example of Gothic house architecture has seven gables, five double chimneys, and seven marble fireplaces. It is furnished throughout as left intact by Dr. and Mrs. J.A. Jones and their children, who lived here 101 years.

Louis Bromfield, native of Mansfield and Pulitzer Prize-winner, played at Oak Hill as a child. His memories of the home became part of his 1924 novel, "The Green Bay Tree."

On display are the original furniture, china, light fixtures, and other artifacts left behind from 1864 to about 1965. Owned by Richland County, this house museum is operated by the Richland County Historical Society.

Photography is permitted, but no flash. You'll find free parking in front of the building.

Visiting hours: Apr. 1–Dec. 31, Sun. only, 2:00 PM to 5:00 PM. Admission is $3.00 adults and youths, $1.00 children 6–12, free to those under 6. Group tours are offered with two weeks' notice.

A special event is scheduled almost every month. Hours are 1:00 PM to 5:00 PM during special events and during the Christmas season.

Address: 310 Spring Mill St., Mansfield, OH 44903. Mail to: Richland County Hist. Soc., 334 Oak Hill Place, Mansfield, OH 44902. Phone: 419–524–1765.

Mansfield:
Ohio State Reformatory

Its cornerstone laid in Nov., 1886, the Ohio State Reformatory (OSR) in Mansfield remains one of the state's most impressive buildings. Architect Levi Scofield designed it "to resemble medieval chateaux and castles," says the brochure. The idea was "to provide a transcendent religious experience, reforming the behaviour of young male prisoners."

Closed in 1990 because of obsolescence, and listed in 1983 on the National Register of Historic Places, this prison is noted for its East Cell Block. Listed in the Guinness Book of World Records, it houses the world's largest free-standing steel cell block, which rises six tiers (stories).

Four motion pictures have had scenes shot in the OSR. They are "Harry and Walter Go to New York," " Tango and Cash," " Shawshank Redemption," and "Air Force One."

The building's cells blocks and warden's residence are open for touring May 16 through Oct. 31, Sun. only, 1:00 PM to 4:00 PM. Admission is $5.00 a person. Group tours are available with advance reservations.

The Mansfield Reformatory Preservation Society is starting a small museum within the prison. On display will be items such as historic photos, prisoner uniforms, and other memorabilia.

Photography, including use of flash, is allowed. There's free parking on the grounds.

Each year, the Preservation Society holds a "Haunted Halloween" event for adults. Parking for that event costs $1.00 a car.

Address: Reformatory Road, Mansfield, OH 44906. Mail to: P.O. Box 8625, Mansfield, OH 44906. Phone: 419-522-2644. Fax: 419-524-5062.

Maple Heights:
Little Red Schoolhouse Museum

Built in 1871, this red-brick building was a one-room school for children of the earliest residents of Bedford Township. The building houses many items of general historic interest, including:

* Fourteen composite pictures of Maple Heights High School graduating classes, beginning with the Class of 1928

* The PBX switchboard from the old Maple Heights fire station

* The cast-iron ID plaque from the old Dunham Rd. bridge

* A 150-year-old square grand piano

* Household tools, equipment, and personal treasures donated by longtime residents of Maple Heights.

Administerd by the Maple Heights Historical Society, the museum is open June 1 through Sept. 30, Mon. and Wed., 7:00 PM to 9:00 PM, and on the second Sun. of every month, 1:00 PM to 4:00 PM. An annual open house takes place during the last weekend of June. Group tours at other times by appointment can be arranged.

Admission is free. Photography, including use of flash, is allowed. You'll find ample free parking nearby.

The museum is at 5810 Dunham Rd. at the corner of Rockside in Maple Heights. Mailing address: Maple Heights Historical Society, P.O. Box 37103, Maple Heights, OH 44137. Phone: 216-662-2851.

Massillon:
Five Oaks Historic Home

Built in 1894 by Mr. and Mrs. J. Walter McClymonds, this large residence includes elements of Gothic, Tudor, and other styles in its architecture. The three floors contain stone and wood carvings, a ballroom, a billiard room in Moroccan leather, stained glass windows, a sweeping staircase, and other attractions.

Operated by the Massillon Women's Club, and owned by the Massillon Heritage Foundation, Inc., this opulent house museum is open for guided tours Sept. 1–June 30, by reservation only, for groups of 15 or more. From July 1–Aug. 31, guided tours for individuals and groups are given on July 11 and 18, and on Aug. 1, 15, 22, and 29.

Special events, including an ice-cream social and fashion show, are held during the summer. Luncheons or dinners for groups of 25 or more may be arranged Sept.1–June 30. For details, call or write.

Admission is $4.00 adults and seniors, $1.00 students 6–17. Preschool children and Foundation members get in free.

There's free parking on adjacent streets. No photography allowed.

Address: 210 Fourth St. NE, Massillon, OH 44646. Phone: 330-833-4896.

Massillon:
Massillon Museum

A varied assortment of exhibits with emphasis on local and regional history and art is the attraction at this 29,000-sq.·

ft. museum in downtown Massillon. Displayed on two floors are comprehensive collections of antique furniture, quilts, china, clothing, sports photos, and the Immel Circus collection.

The last-named collection is a 100-sq.-ft. miniature replica of a complete circus, created by Dr. Robert M. Immel as a life-long hobby. The replica contains a total of 2,620 pieces, most of them carved from wood. Also part of the exhibit are hundreds of historic circus photos and memorabilia donated by Dr. Immel.

The sports photos show well-known Massillon teams and individual players dating from 1894 through the 1930s. Included are prints depicting the city's first high-school football team, the 1905 Tiger pro football team, and teams and players in basketball, baseball, and tennis.

Other exhibits have featured Japanese kimonos and art prints, vintage motorcycles, and valuable Ansel Adams photo prints.

The museum puts on a number of special events, including a show of antique and classic cars, "Island Reggae Party," and pig roast. They also sponsor the Stark County artists exhibition and a number of holiday parties, plus adults' and children's art classes and adult history discussions.

The museum is open year around, six days a week, Tues. through Sun. Closed Mon. Hours are 9:30 AM to 5:00 PM Tues.-Sat., and 2:00 PM to 5:00 PM Sun. Closed on major U.S. holidays.

The Massillon Museum is funded by local property taxes. Admission is free. Group tours can be arranged by appointment. Photography is allowed in some areas; check at the front desk. There's free parking on nearby lots and streets.

Address: 121 Lincoln Way East, Massillon, OH 44646. Phone: 330-833-4061. Fax: 330-833-2925.

Lincoln Way (SR 172) runs east and west through Massillon. You can get onto it from SR 21 and Lilian Gish Blvd. on the west. From the northeast, take SR 241 (Wales Road) south to Lincoln Way, and turn right (west).

Mayfield Village:
Mayfield Township Hist. Soc. Museum

Located in the Bennett-Van Curen Historic House, this
museum opened in 1989. Containing over 12 furnished
rooms, the 30-ft. x 65-ft. building was erected in 1847
by blacksmith Jacob Bennett, and expanded in 1870 by the
George Bennett family. Over the years, the building also
has housed a dentist office, beauty shop, and other busi-
nesses.

The building's original site was at Wilson Mills and SOM
Center Rds. Preservationists moved it about one mile north
on SOM Center in 1987. Placed on a 3/4-acre lot, the
museum displays room furnishings from the early 1800's
through about 1930. Also of special note are a horse-drawn
hearse, a collection of wedding gowns from the 1800's to
the present, and historic items from an early dairy.

Special events at the museum include an annual ice-
cream social, an annual turkey raffle, and a bi-annual quilt
show.

The museum is open year around on Mondays from 10:00
AM to 2:00 PM, and on the third Sunday of every month
from 1:00 PM to 4:00 PM. Special tours can be arranged
at these or other times.

Admission fees are $3.00 adults and seniors, 50 cents
each for children and teenagers in school groups. Children
under 6 get in free with an adult.

Photography, including use of flash, is permitted. There's
free parking on a lot next to the building.

Address: 606 SOM Center Rd., Mayfield Village, OH
44143. Phone: 440-461-0055.

Medina:
John Smart House

This "house museum" was built in 1886 by John Smart, a
Medina businessman who owned an iron foundry. An example of the Queen Anne style, the 14-room house is

furnished in the manner of the late 1800's and early 1900's. Outstanding items on display:
* A homemade tin bathtub
* Ironstone china made in England, ca. 1845–1856
* Ornate chandeliers and glass panes
* Photo of stagecoach standing on Medina's Court Street, showing stage–driver Hiram V. Hill. Made from original tintype.
* China cabinet in French Empire style
* Piano from Civil War days
* Memorabilia from A.J. Root, local businessman who specialized in making candles from beeswax
* Rococo–style sofa
* Portraits of local residents

The John Smart House is owned and operated by the Medina County Historical Society. Open year around on Tues. and Thurs., 9:30 AM to 5:30 PM, and on the first Sun. of each month, 1:00 PM to 4:00 PM. Closed on major U.S. holidays.

Admission is free; donations requested. No photography allowed. There's free parking nearby.

Address: 206 N. Elmwood St., P.O. Box 306, Medina, OH 44256. Phone: 330–722–1341.

Mentor:
Garfield National Historic Site

Recently fully restored, this historic home accurately shows the living conditions of President James A. Garfield and his family during the period 1880 to 1904. The site is operated by the Western Reserve Historical Society, Cleveland, and is owned by the National Park Service.

On the grounds here are the 14–room main house, carriage house, and two outbuildings. About 80 percent of the artifacts in the main house are original Garfield family possessions. A library in the house shows some of the President's books, papers, and personal letters.

A visitor center is contained in the 1893 carriage house, behind the main house. Here you'll find engravings and photos depicting scenes from Garfield's political career, plus documents, clothing, and funeral memorabilia. An 18-min. video film describes his life and career. A museum store offers presidential and Victorian-era souvenirs and memorabilia.

The site is open seven days a week, year around. Hours are: Mon.-Sat. 10:00 AM to 5:00 PM, Sun. 12:00 noon to 5:00 PM. Admission fees: $6.00 adults, $5.00 seniors, $4.00 children 6-12. WRHS members and children under 6 get in free.

There's free parking next to the facility. Group and special tours can be arranged. Photography, including use of flash, is permitted.

For more details, write to: Garfield National Historic Site, 8095 Mentor Ave., Mentor, OH 44060. Phone: 440-255-8722. Fax: 440-255-8545.

Mentor:
Lake County History Center

Located in Shadybrook, once the summer home of Arthur and Reba Baldwin, the Lake County History Center sits on a 15-acre estate that also includes a craft barn, an 1803 log cabin, a replica of a one-room schoolhouse, and Indian archaeological digs. The house itself contains 3,800 sq. ft. of exhibit space on two floors. The property is owned and operated by the Lake County Historical Society.

On display in the museum are furniture, utensils, toys, and other items from the County's early days. In addition to permanent exhibits, the museum shows temporary, rotating exhibits on a variety of topics. A special exhibit shows a large collection of music boxes made between 1870 and 1900.

This facility is open Apr. 1-Nov. 30, six days a week. Hours are Tues.-Fri. 10:00 AM to 5:00 PM, Sat. and Sun. 1:00 PM to 5:00 PM. Closed Mon. and on major U.S. holidays.

Admission is free. The museum allows photography, but no flash. There's free parking on-site.

Address: 8610 King Memorial Rd., Mentor, OH 44060. Phone: 440-255-8979.

SECTION 5 -- MIDDLEFIELD
THROUGH ORRVILLE

Middlefield:
Batavia Inn

Built in 1818 by Isaac Thompson, this two-story frame "house museum" has served at various times as a private residence, boarding house, hospital, and town meeting hall. "Batavia" was the name of this community before it became Middlefield.

Listed on the National Register of Historic Places, Batavia Inn is owned and operated by the Middlefield Historical Society. Restored and in excellent condition, the house holds many furniture pieces, stoves, drapes, and other furnishings from the early 1900's. On display are an old weaving loom and platen-type printing press, plus collections of antique cameras, medical instruments, and other artifacts. Upon appointment, you may access a library of history books pertaining to the region.

Batavia Inn is open year around by appointment only. Admission is free; donations welcome.

There's free parking behind the museum. No photography allowed.

Address: 14979 S. State St., Middlefield, OH 44062. Phone: 440-632-0400.

(Note: Also see the Middlefield Railroad Depot Museum nextdoor.)

Middlefield:
Middlefield Railroad Depot Museum

Located next to the Batavia Inn on S. State St., this restored 1920 depot has exhibits of old B&O lanterns, freight carts, oil cans, and many other railroad artifacts. Middlefield formerly was on a B&O local line that connected Warren, Niles, Middlefield, Chardon, Painesville, Fairport, and other towns.

At one end of the depot is a working, mint-condition soda fountain, where the custodian serves ice-cream cones, sundaes, and sodas. The 1910 fountain, counter, and allied equipment come from a former family-owned drugstore in nearby Byesville, Ohio.

Photography, including use of flash, is allowed. There's free parking next to the museum.

Open Memorial Day to Labor Day, Thurs.-Tues., 2:00 PM to 8:00 PM. Closed on Wed. and national holidays.

Address: 14979 S. State St., Middlefield, OH 44062. Phone: 440-632-0400.

Milan:
Edison's Birthplace Museum

Thomas A. Edison, inventor of the incandescent light bulb, phonograph, and many other devices that made our lives better, was born in this house in 1847. One of seven children, he made his mark in the world with 1,093 American patented inventions.

Restored and furnished as it was in 1847, the museum features a collection of rare Edison memorabilia. These include examples of his early inventions, documents, and family mementoes. Notable are his electric pen, chalk telephone receiver, wireless induction telegraph, and ni-cad battery.

The museum is open Apr. 1-Dec. 31 on various days and at various times. In Feb., Mar., Nov., and Dec., open by appointment only. Closed in Jan., on Mon., and on Easter Sunday. Write or call for details.

Admission: $5.00 adults, $4.00 seniors, $2.00 children 6-12. Children under 6 get in free with an adult. Guided tours lasting 45 minutes are the norm; special group tours and rates can be arranged.

Photography is permitted in the museum, but no flash. There is free parking on the street in front.

Address: 9 Edison Dr., P.O. Box 451, Milan, OH 44846. Phone: 419-499-2135. Fax: 419-499-3241.

Website: www.tomedison.org.

Directions: From the Ohio Turnpike, take Exit 118 south to Milan. Turn east on Church St. (SR 113), and follow signs to the museum. (Also see the Milan Historical Museum.)

Milan:
Milan Historical Museum

During the early and mid-1800's, Milan thrived as a canal port town and boatbuilding center. Reflecting the prosperity of those days is the Milan Historical Museum, a complex of seven buildings on a one-acre site with tended grounds and gardens.

Included in the museum complex are brick houses from 1843 and 1846, a Toy and Doll House, general store, blacksmith shop, and carriage shed. A gift shop offers souvenirs. The houses are furnished after the style of the mid-1800's. The Edna Roe Newton Memorial Building houses international collections of art objects collected from around the world.

Noted collections here include the Mowry Glass Exhibit, over 400 dolls, and photos and information about Milan's canal days.

The museum is open Apr. 1 through Oct. 31, on various days, at various hours. Open by appointment only in Feb., Mar., Nov., and Dec. Closed Jan., Mon., Easter, and Labor Day weekend. Call or write for details.

No photography is permitted. There's free parking on the street in front of the site.

Admission is free; donations of $2.00 a person are requested. Special group tours are offered, and the museum conducts special programs throughout the year.

Address: 10 Edison Dr., P.O. Box 308, Milan, OH 44846. Phone: 419-499-2968. Fax: 419-499-9004. Website: www.milanohio.com.

(Note: Also see Edison's Birthplace Museum in Milan.)

118

Millersburg:
Victorian House Museum

This 28-room mansion, a good example of the Queen Anne
style of architecture, was built in 1902 by L.H. Brightman,
a Cleveland industrialist. It is listed on the National Register
of Historic Places. Highlights of a self-guided tour may
include:
  * A white-oak staircase with 78 hand-turned spindles
and carved acorn finials
  * Leaded stained-glass windows
  * Ornate gas/electric chandeliers
  * Carved furnishings and rich fabrics, all in the Victorian
style
Of special interest among the rooms are turn-of-the-
century law and medical offices, a child's room filled with
antique toys, and a sewing room containing Victorian
dresses. Also see a music room with a variety of old instruments, and a room displaying Civil War artifacts.
Victorian House is open May 1 through Oct. 31, Tues.-
Sun., 1:30 PM to 4:00 PM. Closed on Mon. and major
U.S. holidays. Group and busload tours can be scheduled
with advance notice.
Admission: $3.00 adults and seniors, $1.00 youths 12-
18. Children under 12 get in free with an adult. Special
group rates are available.
Photography is not allowed. You'll find free parking behind
the building.
Address: 484 Wooster Rd., P.O. Box 126, Millersburg,
OH 44654. Phone: 330-674-3975.
Directions: Victorian House is about four blocks north of
SR 39, just off SR 83.

Moreland Hills:
Garfield Birthsite

Not yet a full-fledged museum, the Village Hall of Moreland Hills contains an exhibit of memorabilia concerning the
birthsite and childhood of President James A. Garfield (b.

1831, d. 1881). On display are pictures and various artifacts from his early years. A statue of young Garfield stands to the north of the Hall. The Moreland Hills Historical Society plans to construct a replica of the log cabin in which he was born and grew up.

Garfield's personal history is a remarkable story of success in pioneer Ohio. The last president born in a log cabin, he attended school on a corner of the Garfield farm, and worked for a while as a mule-driver on the Ohio & Erie Canal. After attending various schools, including Williams College, he was elected to the Ohio Senate. He also joined the Union Army, and rose to Major General of Volunteers.

Later, Garfield served in the U.S. House of Representatives, and was elected president in 1880. He was shot in July, 1881, and died in Sept. of that year.

The display in the Village Hall is accessible year around, Mon.-Fri., 9:00 AM to 4:00 PM. Closed on weekends and major U.S. holidays.

Admission is free. You'll find free parking next to the Hall. Photography is permitted outdoors but not indoors, except in special cases.

Address: 4350 SOM Center Rd., Moreland Hills, OH 44022. Phone: 440-247-7282.

(Also see the Garfield National Memorial Site in Mentor, Ohio.)

Mount Pleasant:
Mount Pleasant Historical Center

Originally a Quaker settlement, Mount Pleasant in Jefferson County has preserved six historic buildings in their town center. Five are owned by the local Historical Society; a sixth is owned by the Ohio Historical Society. The local Historical Society operates all six.

In addition, there's a former Quaker Free Labor Store. Now privately owned and occupied as a residence, it was originally two structures. The free-labor store sold only goods and merchandise that was the product of free citizens. Benjamin Lundy, who lived here, was a noted abolitionist and author.

The six museum buildings are:

1. Burriss Store. Served the public from 1895 to 1971. Shelves on one side display the kinds of items sold here in the past. The store now offers souvenirs and gift items.

2, Tin Shop. Built in 1840, made tin products until 1974. See original equipment and tools. A volunteer tinsmith puts on demonstrations for groups on tour.

3. Historical Center. Built in 1856, was a bank, then a Masonic clubhouse. Since 1964, has housed a collection of historic artifacts, clothing, old photos, documents, and genealogical records of the area.

4. Elizabeth House Mansion Museum. Red brick home build in 1835 by John Gill, owner of a silk mill. Furnished with antiques and collectibles of the area. You can tour nine rooms.

5. P.L. Bone Store. A log cabin built in 1804 by Enoch Harris; restored in 1993. Named for a Civil War drummer boy who owned a store here.

6. Friends Yearly Meeting House from 1814. Quaker meeting hall has walls 24 in. thick, laid in the Flemish Bond style. Pews are of poplar with hand-forged riveting and wooden mortise joints. Holds 2,000 people. Owned by the Ohio Historical Society. Features a large wall that could be raised and lowered to separate the men from the women during business meetings.

Open Apr. to Dec., by appointment only. Admission: $7.00 adults, $4.00 children 5-18. Children under 5 get in free. Discounts for groups of 20 or more.

Limited photography permitted; check with your tour guide. There is free parking in the Historic District.

Address: Mt. Pleasant Historic District, P.O. Box 35, Mt. Pleasant, OH 43939. Phone: 740-769-2893 or 740-769-2020.

Mount Vernon:
Dan Emmett House

Daniel Decatur Emmett (b. 1815, d. 1904) was father of the American minstrel show. He composed many popular songs of the middle and late 1800's, including "Dixie Land," "Old Dan Tucker," and "Blue Tail Fly."

Built by Dan's father, a veteran of the War of 1812, the house is decorated with period furniture, wallpaper, fixtures, etc. You may tour the house during special local festivals, and at other times by appointment. Call or write for details.

Photography, including use of flash, is permitted. There's free parking on nearby streets.

Museum address: South Main St., Mount Vernon, OH 43050. Phone: 740-393-5247. Mail to: Knox County Hist. Soc., P.O. Box 522, Mount Vernon, OH 43050.

Mount Vernon:
Knox County Agricultural Museum

Located on the Knox County Fairgrounds, this museum shows the county's farm and home lifestyle in the 1800's and early 1900's. The museum contains more than 3,000 historic items, including a Conestoga wagon, horse-drawn hearse, 1936 Farmall tractor, cream separator, butter churns, and many small farm tools.

The museum complex is comprised of the large main building, a one-room schoolhouse, an 1881 log cabin, and a former house for wild animals.

You may visit the museum during the Knox County Fair, when other events are held at the fairgrounds, and at other times by appointment. Admission is free.

Photography, including use of flash, is permitted. You'll find ample free parking on fairgrounds lots.

Address: Knox County Fairgrounds, P.O. Box 171, Mount Vernon, OH 43050. Phone: 740-397-1423. The fairgrounds is located just north of town on SR 3.

Mount Vernon:
Knox County Hist. Soc. Museum

Opened in 1987, this facility focuses on the domestic and industrial history of the county. In addition to furnished period rooms, the museum contains displays of light and heavy machinery and other products made locally.

Further, the collections here encompass Indian and archaeological artifacts, telephones, musical instruments, toys, and many others. Highlights include four early Cooper steam-powered farm tractors, and personal effects of Daniel Decatur Emmett, a famous local composer.

The archives contain photographs, genealogical records, newspaper files, and military records. Also included are extensive files on the Cooper companies and other local industries.

The museum is open year around on Wed. 6:00 PM to 8:00 PM, and Thurs.-Sun. 2:00 PM to 4:00 PM. Closed on Mon., Tues., and major holidays.

Admission is free; donations and memberships are encouraged. No photography allowed. There's free parking on the grounds.

Address: 997 Harcourt Rd., Mount Vernon, OH 43050. Mail to: P.O. Box 522, Mount Vernon, OH 43050. Phone: 740-393-5247.

New Philadelphia:
Schoenbrunn Village

Founded on May 3, 1772, as a Moravian mission to the Delaware Indians, Schoenbrunn was the first Christian settlement in Ohio. Today the village has been restored to appear much as it did over 220 years ago.

Included are 17 reconstructed log buildings, the original cemetery, and 2.5 acres of planted fields. A museum near the village tells the story of the Delaware and the Moravian missionaries. Among the exhibits are several 18th-Century books, artifacts excavated at the site, and the original mission bell.

123

Schoenbrunn Village is open Memorial Day weekend through Labor Day, Mon.–Sat. 9:30 AM to 5:00 PM, and Sun. 12:00 noon to 5:00 PM. After Labor Day, open to Oct. 31, Sat. 9:30 AM to 5:00 PM, and Sun. 12:00 noon to 5:00 PM.

Admission: $5.00 adults and youths 12–18, $4.50 seniors, $1.25 children 6–12. Children under 6 get in free with an adult. Group tours and special rates can be arranged.

Photography, including use of flash, is permitted. There's free parking on the site, and space for buses.

Address: Schoenbrunn Village, E. High Ave. (SR 259), P.O. Box 129, New Philadelphia, OH 44663. Phone: 330–339–3636 or in Ohio 800–752–2711.

Newark:
National Heisey Glass Museum

From 1896 to 1957, A.H. Heisey & Co., Newark, OH, produced fine glassware for household and decorative uses. This museum, set up in an 1831 Greek Revival building and an addition, displays more than 5,000 outstanding examples of Heisey glassware. Also on exhibit are molds, tools, etching plates, drawings, factory designs, and other artifacts from the company's history.

The museum is open year around, Tues.–Sat. 10:00 AM to 4:00 PM, and Sun. 1:00 PM to 4:00 PM. Closed on Mon. and major U.S. holidays.

No photography permitted. There is parking in front of the museum and on nearby streets. A shop in the building offers glass reproductions from Heisey molds, books, and souvenirs.

Admission: $2.00 adults and seniors. Children under 18 and members get in free. Group tours and special rates are offered.

Address: 169 W. Church St., Veterans Park, Newark, OH 43055. Phone: 740–345–2932.

Newark:
Sherwood-Davidson House Museum

Administered by the Licking County Historical Society, the Newark Historical District includes the 1842 Avery Downer House, 1835 Buckingham Meeting House, 1907 Webb House, and 1815 Sherwood-Davidson House. The first two are available for special events by appointment (call or write for details). The last-named, Sherwood-Davidson House, is a historical "house museum."

On display in this house are artifacts, furnishings, photos and other items from the late 1800's and early 1900's in and around Newark. A truly unique item is the 1860 shower stall with tub. The bather sat in the tub and pulled a handle to release water from a tin pan overhead.

In total, the museum has 5,000 sq. ft. of display area, plus a 1,000-volume library. This contains books and newspapers pertaining to the early history of Newark and Licking County. You may access these for research.

Activities at the museum include guided tours, lectures, film showings, concerts, and traveling and temporary exhibits. You'll find a well-stocked gift shop in the building.

The museum is open Apr.1-Nov. 30, Tues.-Sun., 1:00 PM to 4:00 PM. Closed on Mon. and major U.S. holidays.

Admission is free; donations welcome. Photography, including use of flash, is permitted. There's free parking nearby.

Address: Veterans Park, N. 6th St., P.O. Box 785, Newark, OH 43058. Phone: 614-345-4898.

Newark:
Webb House Museum

Mrs. Shirley Webb lived in this 1907 house until her death in 1976. Preserved as she left it, the house reflects a style of living from the 1920's and 1930's. Her furniture, decorations, furnishings, utensils, and antique collections are all in place, including original paintings, samplers, and pieces of metalwork done by relatives and friends.

125

Outside, the perennial and rose gardens, along with a water-garden pool, are being restored to their original condition.

The museum and grounds are open Apr. 1-Dec. 31, on Thurs., Fri., and Sun., 1:00 PM to 4:00 PM. A special Christmas open house is held during the first weekend of Dec.

Admission is free, but tour-groups of 10 persons or more pay $1.00 apiece. Tours can be arranged with advance notice.

No photography permitted in the museum. You'll find free parking behind the building.

Address: 303 Granville St., Newark, OH 43055. Phone: 740-345-8540. E-mail: webbhouse@nextek.net.

Newcomerstown:
Temperance Tavern Museum

The Turtle Tribe of the Delaware Nation lived in 100 cabins here before moving west to Three Rivers in the late 1770's. The first pioneer farmers arrived in 1803, and settlement began in 1814 by New Jersey pioneers.

This historical museum is housed in the 1841 Temperance Tavern, a local landmark for over a century and a half. Devoted to the history of Newcomerstown and the surrounding area, the museum has permanent, temporary, and touring exhibits of Indian artifacts, antique furniture, period (1827-1930) costumes, remains of a giant woolly mammoth, and memorabilia of Cy Young and Woody Hayes. Activities include guided tours and film showings.

The museum is open year around, Tues.-Sat., 10:00 AM to 3:00 PM, and Sun., 1:00 PM to 4:00 PM. Closed on Mon. and major U.S. holidays.

Admission is $1.00; children under 12 -- 50 cents. Tour groups qualify for special rates. Reservations for group tours should be made in advance.

Photography, including use of flash, is permitted. You'll find free parking in front and on nearby streets.

126

Address: 221 W. Canal St., P.O. Box 443, Newcomerstown, OH 43832. Phone: 614-498-7735.

Directions: From I-77, get off at SR 36. Head west to the first blinker lights, then right on Canal St. The museum is one-half block past the post office.

Niles:
McKinley Birthplace Memorial

This handsome, 232-ft. x 136-ft., Greek Classic structure has three elements: a central court featuring a 10-ft. statue of Pres. William McKinley, a library wing, and a museum wing. The museum contains memorabilia from McKinley's early life in Niles, plus Civil War artifacts and many items from his presidential campaign and days in office.

Born in Niles on Jan. 29, 1843, McKinley distinguished himself in the Civil War. He was the first to employ campaign buttons and other promotional items during a presidential campaign. McKinley was assassinated in Buffalo in 1901.

The museum and library are open year around on Mon.-Thurs., 9:00 AM to 8:00 PM; Fri. and Sat., 9:00 AM to 5:30 PM; and Sun., 1:00 PM to 5:00 PM. Closed on Sun. from June 1-Aug. 31, and on major U.S. holidays.

Admission is free. Group tours can be arranged. Photography is permitted for personal use, but no flash. There's free parking in back of the building.

Address: 40 N. Main St., Niles, OH 44446. Phone: 330-652-1704. Website: www.mckinley.lib.oh.us.

(Note: Also see the McKinley Museum in Canton, and several museums in Youngstown, which is near Niles.)

North Canton:
Hoover Historical Center

Located in the historic boyhood home of company founder William H. "Boss" Hoover, this museum and grounds have displays that trace the history of the family and development of Hoover vacuum-cleaner technology. Period settings from 1850 to 1950 enhance the seven open rooms. Herb gardens outside add yet another dimension. There's a gift shop on the premises.

Thought to be the most complete collection of vacuum cleaners in the world, this one shows the first Hoover, Model O, introduced in 1908. Also on display are manual cleaners from the late 1800's and early 1900's, and many electric models. In all, some 75 cleaners are exhibited.

The museum and grounds are open to the public year around, Tues.-Sun., 1:00 PM to 5:00 PM. Closed on Mon. and major U.S. holidays.

The Center hosts several special events throughout the year. They include garden tours, "Halloween Storytelling Festival," and "Christmas Open House." Write or call for details.

Admission is free. Advance reservations are required for groups of 10 or more persons.

Photography is permitted throughout the Center. There's ample free parking on the grounds, including spaces for handicapped and buses.

Owned and operated by The Hoover Co., the Historical Center is located inside Hoover Park at 1875 Easton St. NW, North Canton, OH 44720. Phone: 330-499-0287. Fax: 330-494-4725.

North Canton:
MAPS Air Museum

"MAPS" stands for "Military Air Preservation Society." A group of aircraft enthusiasts, mostly veterans of World War II and the Korean War, they volunteer their time, skills, and energy to restoring vintage warplanes. Headquartered in a former Ohio Air National Guard maintenance building on the western edge of Akron-Canton Airport, the Society and its museum opened to the public in Sept., 1990.

Now, on their 12,000-sq.-ft. of floor space, you can see two Douglas SBD Dauntless dive-bombers being re--

stored. Also being restored here are a Martin B-26 Marauder bomber (one of only six still existing), a Polish-built MIG-17F fighter, a Bell P-39Q Aircobra fighter, and a Curtiss P-40N Warhawk fighter.

Other aircraft on display, in the restoration area and outdoors on a tarmac, include two Bell military helicopters, a Beechcraft SNB-5 Expeditor trainer/transport, a Douglas C-47B Skytrain transport, and a North American T-28A Trojan trainer.

The restoration area also contains a fragment from the dirigible Hindenburg, a gondola car from the Goodyear blimp "Spirit of Akron," a Norden bombsight, an operational Link Trainer, and two models of Bofors 40mm anti-aircraft guns. The last-named were built under license in Akron by Firestone.

In the museum display rooms, you'll find historic aviators' uniforms, photos, and aviation artwork. A model airplane room houses over 800 scale-model planes from around the world.

Also part of the facility is a gift shop stocked with model airplane kits, posters, T-shirts, caps, and many other kinds of aviation memorabilia. If you want to do research on military aviation, you can access the Louise Timken Aviation Research Library, stocked with hundreds of books, manuals, old magazine issues, and audio-visual tapes.

The MAPS and its museum hold fund-raising events such as a Winter Chili Lunch or Spaghetti Dinner, Hangar Dance, and aircraft fly-ins. Visits by a B-17 and B-24 are planned for 1999.

The museum is open May 1 to Oct. 31, on Sun. 12:00 noon to 4:00 PM; Mon. 9:00 AM to 4:00 PM; Wed. 6:00 PM to 9:00 PM; and Sat. 8:00 AM to 4:00 PM. From Nov. 1 to Apr. 30, hours are: Wed. 6:00 to 9:00 PM, and Sat. 8:00 AM to 4:00 PM. The staff will arrange special tours and group-tours for other days and times, on request.

Photography, including use of flash, is allowed. Admission is free; donations welcome.

The MAPS Air Museum is located at 5359 Massillon Rd. (SR 241), North Canton, OH 44720. Phone: 330-896-6332. The entrance is about one mile south of Greensburg

Rd., on the east side of Massillon Rd. There's a Macedonian Orthodox church just north of the entrance.

North Olmsted:
Frostville Museum

In the 1830's, Elias Frost, an early settler in the area, applied for a postal station in his name. Even after the official postoffice name was changed, the Frostville designation for the surrounding area remained.

A grouping of five original, historic frame buildings, this museum helps you to imagine farm life in the early 1800's and later in Olmsted Township. On display are antique farm implements, kitchen tools, and home furnishings. In a barn attached to the General Store you can view an 1830 Hearst, a 1929 Seagraves pumper, and many other historic items.

The Frostville Museum is open from Memorial Day through Oct. 31, on Sun. only, from 2:00 PM to 5:00 PM. Admission is free. No photography allowed. Free parking on the grounds.

Each March, the Olmsted Historical Society holds a pancake breakfast on the grounds. Write or call for details.

Address: 24101 Cedar Point Rd., North Olmsted, OH 44138. Mailing address: 18 Elgin Oval, Olmsted Twp., OH 44138. Phone: 440-777-0059 or 440-235-4216.

Norwalk:
Firelands Museum

During the Revolutionary War, many residents of Connecticut had their homes burned down by British soldiers. After the war, these citizens petitioned their state and won a tract of 500,000 acres on the western edge of the "Connecticut Western Reserve," along the south shore of Lake Erie. The "fire sufferers" sent surveyors in 1808 to lay out the tract into townships.

Settlers began arriving in 1809. Today the Firelands Museum preserves and displays memorabilia from those days and later in an 1836 frame house. This was built originally by Samuel Preston, a local newspaper editor, for his daughter Lucy and her husband Frederick Wickham. Preston ran his newspaper on the second floor.

On display are collections of firearms, the original compass belonging to surveyor Jabez Wright, links and chains belonging to surveyor Almon Ruggles, early maps of the area, and a copy of the Treaty of Fort Industry. This was concluded in 1805 at the site of present-day Toledo.

Also on display are period furniture, gowns, textiles, glassware, toys, pioneer implements, Indian artifacts, and Civil War items. Some of the rooms in the house are furnished as period settings.

Possibly the oldest museum in Ohio (est. 1857), this facility is open in Apr., May, Sept., Oct., and Nov. on Sat. and Sun., 12:00 noon to 4:00 PM. The museum also is open June 1–Aug. 31 on Tues.–Sun., 12:00 noon to 5:00 PM. Closed Dec. 1–Mar. 31 except by appointment. Closed on major U.S. holidays.

There's parking behind the museum and on nearby streets. Photography, including use of flash, is permitted.

Admission: $3.00 adults, $2.50 seniors, $2.00 youths 12–18. Children under 12 get in free with an adult. Group rates and special tours can be arranged. School groups get in free.

Address: 4 Case Ave., P.O. Box 572, Norwalk, OH 44857. Phone: 419–668–6038.

Directions: Norwalk is about seven miles south of the Ohio Turnpike (I–80 and I–90) via SR 250. Get off at Exit 7. Case Ave. is at the western edge of the West Main St. historic district.

Norwich:
National Road/Zane Grey Museum

The highlight of this unusual museum is a 136-ft. diorama depicting the construction and use of The National Road, later to become part of U.S. 40. The Road began in 1806, when Congress authorized construction of a highway from Cumberland, Md., to the Ohio River. At first the Road consisted of beds dug 12" to 18" by hand, then filled with crushed rock and rolled flat.

Serving as the main highway for opening our new West, the Road eventually reached Vandalia, Ill. Construction was ended after 29 years and 600 miles, but later the Road became the eastern leg of U.S. 40, a transcontinental national route that today ends in Salt Lake City, Utah, and joins I-80. U.S. 40 has carried everything from foot traffic, mules, and horses to Conestoga wagons, stage-coaches, bicycles, autos, and trucks.

In nearby Zanesville, author Zane Grey celebrated the opening West in dozens of novels, from which over 100 movies were made. One of the best-know is "Riders of the Purple Sage." The Zane Grey portion of this museum shows a collection of his trophies, manuscripts, first editions, and other memorabilia.

Other parts of the building display historic vehicles used on the National Road, and many examples of art pottery made in the area. During the early 20th Century, Zanesville was the center of a sizeable pottery industry.

This museum is open Mar. 1 through Nov. 30, on various days, at various hours. Open 12:00 noon to 5:00 PM on all holidays but Thanksgiving. Write or call for details.

Photography, including use of flash, is permitted. There's free parking on the grounds.

Admission: $5.00 adults, $4.50 seniors, $1.25 children 6-12. Children under 6 get in free with an adult. Group rates and special tours can be arranged.

Address: National Road/Zane Grey Museum, 8850 East Pike, U.S. 40, Norwich, OH 43767. Phone: 740-872-3143 or 800-752-2602.

Oberlin:
Allen Memorial Art Museum

Owned and operated by Oberlin College, this facility was founded as a teaching museum, primarily for art students at the College and for local citizens. The permanent collection includes over 11,000 objects from most periods.

Outstanding holdings include 17th–Century Dutch and Flemish paintings, European paintings of the late 19th and early 20th Centuries, Old Master and Japanese prints, and contemporary American paintings. On display are early works of Monet, Mondrian, Picasso, Warhol, and Domen–ichino.

The museum frequently shows traveling exhibitions, and offers a variety of programs for children. A museum store called "Uncommon Objects" offers products based on items in the Museum, plus original works by contemporary artists.

The museum is open year around, six days a week. Hours: Tues.–Sat. 10:00 AM to 5:00 PM, Sun. 1:00 PM to 5:00 PM. Closed on Mon. and major U.S. holidays.

Admission is free. Photography of some older permanent holdings is permitted, but no flash. Group tours can be arranged. You'll find free parking in front and back of the building.

Address: Allen Memorial Art Museum, Oberlin College, 87 N. Main St., Oberlin, OH 44074. Phone: 440–775–8665. Fax: 440–775–6841. Website: www.oberlin.edu/allenart.

Oberlin:
Oberlin Heritage Center

The Oberlin Historical and Improvement Organization (OHIO) offers guided tours of three sites at the Oberlin Heritage Center, near the center of town. The three are the Monroe House, Little Red Schoolhouse, and Jewett House.

The Monroe House, built in 1866, is a brick Italianate-style edifice owned first by Gen. Giles W. Shurtleff. A Civil War leader for the North, he headed the first African

American regiment from Ohio to serve in the War. Later the deed passed to James and Julia Monroe. Mr. Monroe was an abolitionist and friend of Frederick Douglass, and taught at Oberlin College.

The Little Red Schoolhouse, built in 1836, housed the first public school in town. Restored as a pioneer-era building, it is a favorite of children.

Built in 1884, the Jewett House was home to Frank F. Jewett. He and his wife wrote books on public health and hygiene. The house and barn are on the National Register of Historic Places.

On display in this house is a new exhibit. Called "Aluminum: The Oberlin Connection," it explains the development of aluminum manufacture. Included is a re-creation of Charles M. Hall's 1886 woodshed experiment station.

OHIO offers guided tours one hr. and 15 min. long, on Tues., Thurs., and Sat., at 10:30 AM and 1:30 PM. Open year around, but closed on major U.S. holidays and during the week between Christmas and New Year's.

Many programs and special events are held throughout the year. Write or call for details.

Admission: $4.00 a person for a guided tour of the three buildings. Free to OHIO members and children under 19 accompanied by a parent or guardian. Group tours of 10 or more persons can be arranged at special rates.

Photography, including use of flash, is permitted throughout the tour, with permission of the Executive Director. There's ample free parking in the downtown area and on nearby streets.

Address: OHIO, 73-1/2 S. Professor St., P.O. Box 0455, Oberlin, OH 44074. Phone: 440-774-1700.

Directions: Near downtown Oberlin. Tours begin at the Monroe House, behind the Post Office.

Olmsted Township:
Trolleyville USA

In this museum park, you can take rides on restored electric trolley cars and light-rail urban transit trains. The park contains a restored depot, car barns, and about three miles of track.

Among the vehicles you can ride are a lightweight interurban built for Illinois's Fox River Line in 1923, a single-truck summer car from Philadelphia (ca. 1900), a 1914 Cleveland streetcar, and a two-car interurban train built in 1923 by Pullman for the Chicago, Aurora & Elgin line. The last-named sometimes ran at speeds over 80 mph.

Founded in 1954, Trolleyville, USA, has the corporate name of the Gerald E. Brookins Museum of Electric Railways, Inc. A non-profit corporation, it relies on admission fees, gifts, and grants for its operation.

The park is open May 1 to Nov. 21, on Wed., Fri., Sat., and Sun., at various hours. Call or write for full details.

Admission is $5.00 for adults, $4.00 for seniors and youths 12-18, and $3.00 for children 3-11. Children under 3 get in free with an adult. Admission includes rides on all vehicles operating that day, plus tours.

In the park, you can view displays and tour the car barns, a century-old B&O Berea depot, and a restoration workshop. There's also a picnic area for the public's use.

Photography, including use of flash, is allowed. There's free parking on-site. You can schedule group tours at special rates with advance notice.

Address: 7100 Columbia Rd., Olmsted Township, OH 44138. Phone: 440-235-4725. Trolleyville, USA, is located on Columbia Rd. (SR 252) between I-480 and Bagley Rd.

Orrville:
Orrville Railroad Depot Museum

Operated by the Orrville Railroad Heritage Society, this authentic depot stands at the junction of two former Pennsylvania Railroad lines. The Society owns the interlocking tower that formerly controlled the junction, plus a number of passenger cars and diesel locomotives and a caboose.

The museum, located in the depot, contains displays of railroad memorabilia, including a steam-engine bell. Also in this building is a store that sells souvenirs. A "kiddy train" ride for small children is set up and running during "Depot Days," held on two weekends in June.

Also during Depot Days, and on the Thanksgiving Day weekend, an experienced staff operates short train-rides on the local tracks. These rides last about 15 min. In addition, several times a year the museum conducts longer train excursions to destinations ranging from Sugarcreek, OH, to Niagara Falls, NY. Some excursions run all day or overnight. Call for details on destinations, days, times, and prices.

The museum is open from mid-Apr. to Sept. 30, Sat. only, 11:00 AM to 5:00 PM. Closed on weekends when excursions are being run. (Be sure to phone ahead before you come.)

Admission to the museum is free, but the staff asks for donations. Photography, including use of flash, is permitted. There's free parking next to the depot.

Address: 145 Depot St., P.O. Box 11, Orrville, OH 44667. Phone: 330-683-2426.

(Note: Also see the Orrville Historical Museum nextdoor, and the Toy & Hobby Museum nearby in Orrville.)

Orrville:
Toy and Hobby Museum

Opened in April, 1992, this attraction features collections of over 4,500 imprinted toy trucks in sizes up to 1/16th scale. Also on display are over 10,000 different pencils, 400 vintage toy tractors and implements, and about 1,000 pairs of salt and pepper shakers.

Other exhibits contain Indian artifacts, dolls, teddy bears, and a miniature farm at 1/64th scale.

This museum is open year around on Mon., Fri., and Sat. Hours are: Mon. and Fri., 6:30 PM to 9:00 PM, and Sat., 12:00 noon to 6:00 PM. Open on other days and at other times by appointment.

Admission is $3.00 a person, or $10.00 for a family of any size. Group tours and special rates can be arranged.

Photography, including use of flash, is allowed. There's free parking nearby.

Address: 531 W. Smithville Rd., Orrville, OH 44667. Phone: 330-683-TOYS or 330-683-6421.

Directions: Drive 1/4-mi. west of SR 57 on Smithville Rd., on the north edge of Orrville. The museum is about 3 miles north of U.S. 30, and 13 miles south of I-76.

SECTION 6 -- PAINESVILLE
THROUGH WELLINGTON

Painesville:
Indian Museum of Lake County

Located at the west end of the Lake Erie College campus off Mentor Ave., this museum is administered by the Lake County chapter of the Archaeological Society of Ohio.

Exhibits describe and illustrate the earliest Native American groups living in the Ohio area from about 10,000 BC to 1650 AD. These groups include the Paleo, Archaic, Adena, and Hopewell Moundbuilders, and the Whittlesey Culture. Other exhibits tell of the art, crafts, and people of the Eastern Woodlands, Great Plains, Southwest, Pacific Northwest, and Alaska -- from 1800 to the present.

The museum is open May 1–Aug. 31, Mon.–Fri. 10:00 AM to 4:00 PM, and Sat.–Sun. 1:00 PM to 4:00 PM; also Sept. 1–Apr. 30, Mon.–Fri., 9:00 AM to 4:00 PM; and Sat.–Sun., 1:00 PM to 4:00 PM. Closed on major U.S. holidays and during Lake Erie College's winter and spring breaks. (Call to verify hours open.)

Special activities involve workshops on topics such as identification of Indian artifacts, flintknapping (making tools of flint), and basketmaking. The facility includes a reference library on Indian topics.

Special tours can be arranged for any student or adult group, with advance reservations. A fee is charged.

Admission is $2.00 adults, $1.50 seniors, and $1.00 students. Preschoolers get in free with an adult.

Photography, including use of flash, is permitted. There's free parking near the museum on school lots.

Address: 391 W. Washington St., Painesville, OH 44077. Phone: 440–352–1911.

Directions: In Painesville, find the campus of Lake Erie College, which is just south of Mentor Ave., accessed from Washington St. On the campus, find Kilcawley Hall at the western end of the campus. The Indian Museum is in the basement of this building.

Parma:
Stearns Homestead

An organization called the Parma Area Historical Society seeks to perpetuate the memory of pioneers and early settlers of Parma Township. Part of their effort has gone into preservation and restoration of the Stearns Homestead, a museum which includes an 1848 farmhouse, 1920 house, "Yankee" barn, and working farm.

On display in the farmhouses are original furnishings and implements of the 1800's and early 1900's, plus historical documents and relics. An old-fashioned country store on the grounds sells ice cream, sodas, candy, and craft items. The working farm lets people get acquainted with horses, pigs, sheep, goats, rabbits, and other animals.

The Society holds special events here throughout the year. They include a strawberry and ice cream social, sheep-shearing demonstration, apple and herb festival, and flea market. A special Christmas shop is open in November; call for days and times.

Photography, including use of flash, is allowed throughout the site. There's parking for about 30 cars on the grounds, plus more across the road. Admission is free. Special tours can be arranged.

Stearns Homestead is open from May 30 to Nov. 1, on Sat. and Sun., 1:00 PM to 4:30 PM. The address is 6975 Ridge Rd., Parma, OH 44129. Phone: 440-845-9770.

Port Clinton:
Ottawa County Historical Museum

A general museum covering the history of Ottawa County, this facility has exhibits showing Indian artifacts, dishes, toys, dolls, linens, guns, swords, fossils, and rocks. Also on display are historic photos, paintings, postcards, and books. Clipping files and genealogical records round out the collection.

The museum is open Apr. 1 through Dec. 31, on Tues., Wed., and Thurs., from 1:00 PM to 4:00 PM. Closed Jan.

1 through Mar. 31 and on major U.S. holidays.

Admission is free. The management allows photography, including use of flash. You'll find free parking in front of the building.

Address: 126 W. 3rd St., Port Clinton, OH 43452. Phone: 419-732-2237.

Put-in-Bay:
Lake Erie Islands Museum

Located on South Bass Island, this museum displays a Fourth Order lighthouse lens, 68 ship models, an 8-ft. x 56-ft. mural of the Battle of Lake Erie, an ice-fishing shanty, and memorabilia of Admiral Oliver H. Perry. There are vine-yards and wineries nearby, open for touring.

The museum is open May 15-Sept. 30, seven days a week, 10:00 AM to 6:00 PM. Photography is permitted, but no flash. There's ample free parking on the grounds. Admission is free; donations encouraged.

Address: P.O. Box 25, Put-in-Bay, OH 43456. Phone: 419-285-2804 or 419-285-3814. For directions, ask at the boat dock.

(Also see the Perry Memorial Museum in Put-in-Bay.)

Put-in-Bay:
Perry Memorial Museum

Housed in the Perry's Victory and International Peace Memorial building, this museum commemorates Admiral Perry's victory over the British in the 1812 Battle of Lake Erie. Permanent exhibits contain weapons and equipment from that War, including naval ordnance, plus many litho-graphs and engravings that depict the Lake Erie battle. A 1,000-volume library on the period is available for re-search.

Among the activities are lectures and tours of the entire monument and museum. There's a gift shop on the premises.

Photography, including use of flash, is allowed throughout the facility.

Open: Early Spring and late Fall -- daily, 10:00 AM to 5:00 PM. Late Spring and early Fall -- daily, 10:00 AM to 6:00 PM. Summer: daily, 10:00 AM to 7:00 PM. Also open by appointment during the off-season.

Fees: $3.00 adults (17 and older); others get in free.

Address: 93 Delaware St., P.O. Box 549, Put-in-Bay, South Bass Island, OH 43456. Phone: 419-285-2184. Fax: 419-285-2516.

(Access to South Bass Island is by ferry boat from Port Clinton or Catawba Island.)

Ravenna:
Portage County Hist. Soc. Museum

Housed in an 1828 residence called The Carter House, this museum displays collections pertaining to county history. Included are exhibits of glassware, china, and miscellaneous artifacts, plus archaeological findings from the area. A library holds historical books and records of genealogy. Activities include lectures and guided tours.

Also open for viewing on the Portage County Historical Society's 12-acre grounds is the Lowrie-Beatty Museum, built in the late 1960's in the style of the late 1800's. This museum has historical displays on two floors, plus a meeting area, library, genealogical section, gift shop, and offices.

Other attractions on the grounds are:

* John Campbell Land Office. During the War of 1812, it was used as a hospital and mustering office.

* Mahan New England Barn. A "Yankee barn" ca. 1810.

* Ford Seed Co. Building. Originally a photographer's studio in Garrettsville; now displays Ford Seed Co. memorabilia.

* Army caisson and limber, once used in military funerals.

* Steam traction engine, obtained from the Advance Brumley Co., Battle Creek, Mich.

* Merts and Riddle Co. hearse. This was built in Raven-

na; horse-drawn, made of wood.

* Proehl-Kline Clock Tower. Houses an 1882 Seth Thomas Model 18 clock.

* Lady Justice statue.

* Mantua Glass Factory Site. Archaeological digs are ongoing.

The Carter House museum and other attractions are open year around on Tues. and Thurs., 2:00 PM to 4:00 PM, and Sun., 2:00 PM to 5:00 PM. Tours at other times can be arranged.

Admission is free; donations welcome. No photography allowed inside. There's free parking in front and on nearby streets.

Address: 6549 N. Chestnut St., Ravenna, OH 44266. Phone: 330-296-3523.

Salem:
Salem Hist. Soc. Museum

Specializing in local history, the Salem Museum contains collections of artifacts, photos, and publications pertaining to the town's abolitionist days, the Civil War, and Quaker, Romanian, and Saxon (German) settlers. Also on display are woodworking tools, glass, china, Valentine's Day cards, postcards, kitchen utensils, and toys from Salem's past. The Society maintains a library of books on local and Ohio history, including a few rare books.

You may visit the museum May 1-Oct. 31, Sun. only, 2:00 PM to 4:00 PM, and at other times by appointment. Admission is $2.00 adults, $1.00 children.

Photography, including use of flash, is permitted. There's limited free parking on the street in front.

Address: 208 S. Broadway Ave., Salem, OH 44460. Mailing address: 849 S. Lincoln Ave., Salem, OH 44460. Phone: 330-337-8514.

Sandusky:
Eleutheros Cooke House

The first lawyer in Sandusky, Eleutheros Cooke served
several terms in the Ohio Legislature (1831–1833), and
one term in the U.S. Congress. He drew up the charter for
the Mad River and Lake Erie Railroad, and helped to found
the Firelands Historical Society in Norwalk.

Built in 1833 and 1834, this house contains a variety of
antiques, including furniture, glassware, clocks, porcelain
pieces, and others. The house remains much as it looked
when the last owners lived here in the 1950s. The Ohio
Historical Society owns the house; it is managed by the Old
House Guild of Sandusky.

Eleutheros Cooke House is open six days a week Apr. 1–
Dec. 31; closed on Mon. Hours: Tues.–Sat. 10:00 AM to
3:00 PM, and Sun. 12:00 noon to 3:00 PM. Open Jan. 1
to Mar. 31 by appointment only.

Admission is $4.00 a person. No photography allowed.
There's free parking on-site. Group tours can be arranged.

Address: 1415 Columbus Ave., Sandusky, OH 44870.
Phone: 419-627-0640.

Sandusky:
Follett House Museum

Along with the Sandusky Library, this museum is located in
the former home of Oran Follett, one of the city's founders.
Built in 1834–37, the building is a fine example of Greek
Revival architecture. A "widow's walk" on the roof, acces-
sible to visitors, offers a panoramic view of Sandusky, Lake
Erie, and nearby Johnson's Island.

In the museum are many artifacts from Johnson's Island
Prison, which housed Confederate officers during the Civil
War. Among the artifacts are prison-related letters, diaries,
photos, and drawings. Also on display is a Baltimore-style
quilt made in the 1840s.

The library holds a special collection of archival documents and artifacts for scholarly study of the history of

143

Sandusky and Erie County.

The museum and library are open Apr., May, Sept., Oct., Nov., and Dec. on Sat. and Sun., 12:00 noon to 4:00 PM. Also open in June, July, and Aug., Tues.–Sat., same hours. Closed in Jan., Feb., and Mar., and on major U.S. holidays.

Admission is free. Group tours, including school classes, can be arranged, as can guided tours. Please call ahead for these.

Photography, including use of flash, is permitted for personal use only. You'll find free parking next to the building.

Address: 404 Wayne St., Sandusky, OH 44870. Phone: 419–627–9608. Website: www.sandusky.lib.oh.us.

(While in Sandusky, also see the Eleutheros Cooke House, Sandusky Maritime Museum, and Merry–Go–Round Museum.)

Sandusky:
Merry–Go–Round Museum

Begun in about 580 AD in Europe, the art of the carousel (merry–go–round) and its carved figures came to the U.S. in the late 1800's. During the carousel's "Golden Age," over 7,000 wooden units were built in this country alone. Today, fewer than 150 wooden carousels remain.

Dedicated to saving, preserving, and fostering this venerable art form, the Merry–Go–Round Museum collects and restores individual horse–figures. Housed in a hand-some, 1920's former U.S. Post Office building in down-town Sandusky, the museum contains workshops for carvers and painters, horse–figure displays, and a complete, working carousel that visitors can ride.

One highlight is the simulated, fully equipped workshop of G.A. Dentzell, a Philadelphia carver who in the later 1800's pioneered the art form in this country. Another attraction is a Wurlitzer Model 150 band organ, which provides music for the working carousel. Fine, painted specimens of horse–figures done in the major styles ––

Philadelphia, Coney Island, and County or Country Fair --
are on display.

The museum is open weekends only in Jan. and Feb.;
seven days a week from Memorial Day to Labor Day; and
Wed.-Sun. during other months. Hours are 11:00 AM to
5:00 PM Mon.-Sat., and 12:00 noon to 5:00 PM on Sun.

Admission is $4.00 adults, $3.00 seniors, $2.00 children
4-14. Children under 4 get in free. All those under 14
must be accompanied by an adult.

Group rates and special tours can be arranged. The main
museum hall can be rented for special occasions. Photography, including use of flash, is permitted. You'll find free
parking behind the building, which contains a gift shop.

Address: P.O. Box 718, Sandusky, OH 44870. Phone:
419-626-6111. Fax: 419-626-1297.

Location: At the corner of W. Washington and Jackson Sts.
(SR 6), on the square in downtown Sandusky.

Sandusky:
Sandusky Area Maritime Museum

From the earliest days of Great Lakes navigation, Sandusky's
harbor has been considered the best in the chain. Practically
landlocked, it offers a safe haven during storms, and gives
anchorage room for more vessels than any other harbor on
the Great Lakes.

Sandusky was a major center for freshwater fish supply in
the U.S. For years, fishing was considered the city's main
industry, with exports topping 10 million lbs. annually.
Moreover, before the advent of electric refrigeration, Sandusky was a leader in production of natural ice. After a
winter freeze, hundreds of locals were employed in cutting
and storing ice blocks.

Located just one block from the water, this museum has
displays showing:
 * The history of the Lyman Boat Works
 * Collections of early ice-cutting tools
 * Ship models in various scales

* Many artifacts from ships that served the Port of Sandusky
* Photos showing local, lake–related industies such as boat–building, ice–harvesting, and fishing.

A gift shop in the museum offers items relating to Great Lakes and local maritime activities, including books, T–shirts, coffee mugs, and many others. With advance notice, school classes and other groups can schedule guided tours.

Open Apr. 1–Nov. 30., Tues.–Sat., 1:00 PM to 4:00 PM. Closed on Sun., Mon., major U.S. holidays, and Dec. 1–Mar. 31. Admission is free; donations welcome. Photography, including use of flash, is permitted. There's free parking on a city lot across the street.

Address: 279 E. Market St., Sandusky, OH 44870. Phone: 419–624–0274. Fax: 419–621–9283. Website: www.sanduskymaritime.org. E–mail: SMMuseum @ AOL.com.

Shaker Heights:
Shaker Historical Museum

Opened in 1956, this museum is owned and operated by the Shaker Historical Society. The Tudor mansion occupies a tract where once stood the largest of the North Union Shaker Colony dwellings and an apple orchard.

Religious refugees from England, the Shakers –– named after their body–shaking during religious ceremonies –– believed in communal living, pacifism, confession of sins, and God's "dual personality," male and female. They practiced equality of sexes in all activities, but they also insisted on celibacy among members. This meant their Society could grow only by conversions.

The Shakers excelled in agriculture, marketing, furniture–making, spinning, weaving, and creative design and engineering. Shaker inventions include the clothespin, washing machine, circular saw, flat broom, and rotary oven. Sturdy, light, and simple of line, Shaker furniture and other artifacts remain popular to this day.

The Shaker Historical Museum maintains a permanent collection of Shaker furniture, tools, woven goods, and other artifacts. The focus of the displays is on the contributions and legacy of the North Union Colony. The museum also explains the achievements of the Van Sweringen brothers, including the Terminal Tower in Cleveland.

On the second floor, you'll find a library containing books and archival material concerning the Shakers, early Warrensville history, and the development of Shaker Heights.

This museum is open year around, Tues.-Fri. and Sun., 2:00 PM to 5:00 PM. Closed on Mon., Sat., and major U.S. holidays. Admission is free, though tour-groups may be charged a small fee. There is limited, free parking on the grounds and on S. Park Blvd. No photography is allowed inside the museum.

Address: 16740 S. Park Blvd., Shaker Heights, OH 44120. Phone: 216-921-1201. Fax: 216-921-2615.

Directions: From Lee Rd. (a north-south street), turn east on S. Park Blvd., and go to the fourth driveway on the right.

Sheffield Lake:
103rd Ohio Infantry Museum

Founded in 1972, this is a memorial to the 103rd Ohio Volunteer Infantry Regiment, which fought in the Union Army. A frame house built in 1900 houses collections of Civil War relics, with emphasis on the 103rd. Collections include items such as weapons, uniforms, flags, camp lamps, fife and drum, books, and historic photos.

The building also contains a gift shop, a 300-seat hall, and a 300-volume library of books on Civil War history. These books can be accessed for research. Activities include guided tours, lectures, and showings of videotapes.

Open on request, by appointment. Suggested donations are $1.00 for adults and 50 cents for children 6-18. Children under 6 get in free.

Photography, including use of flash, is permitted. There's free parking on the one–acre grounds.

Address: 5501 E. Lake Rd., Sheffield Lake, OH 44054. Phone: 440–949–2790 or 440–949–2976.

Smithville:
Smithville Historic Sites

Near one another in Smithville are three wooden structures that show graphically the lifestyles of early settlers. Owned and operated by the Smithville Community Historical Society, they are called the "Pioneer Log Cabin," the "Sheller House & Carriage Barn," and the "Mishler Weaving Mill."

A two–story house, the Pioneer Log Cabin illustrates home life in the early 1800's on Ohio's frontier. Of special note are the wooden door–hinges and latches, stone hearth, firewood box that doubled as a guest's bed, candle mold, and kitchen utensils. Upstairs, see the rope beds covered with straw or feather ticks, and woven jacquard coverlets from the 1830's.

The Sheller House, one of Smithville's original log houses, dates from ca. 1850. Owned by G. Sheller, a tailor, it is more "grand" than the Pioneer Log Cabin nextdoor, in that the Sheller House boasts of plastered walls, hand–forged iron box–locks, and windows made of hand–poured glass.

On display downstairs are wooden chairs, tables, and other furniture made by local artisans during the mid–1800's. Upstairs, one room contains artifacts pertaining to Smithville's days as a county center for learning. Another room has furnishings and decorations of a bedroom from the early 1800's.

Beside the Sheller House sits a carriage barn believed to date from the late 19th Century. It may have been a livery for stagecoaches that traveled the Portage Path (now SR 585) between Akron and Wooster.

Two blocks east of the two log houses is the Mishler Weaving Mill. Erected by Swiss immigrant John C. Mishler and his family, it turned out woven rag rugs, dishcloths, bath towels, and washcloths. During the early 1900's, the mill wove cheesecloth and cider-press cloth that was sold worldwide.

Today, members of the local Historical Society continue to weave rugs and cloth on looms well over 100 years old. These items are offered for sale in a small gift shop in the building. Also on sale are postcards, logo patches, and other items. Proceeds help to maintain the building. The mill is open every Wed. afternoon from 1:30 PM to 4:00 PM.

The other two historic structures are open May 1 to Sept. 30, on Sat. and Sun. of the third weekend only, from 2:00 PM to 4:00 PM, and by appointment throughout the year. Tours for individuals, families, or groups can be arranged. The annual Christmas Open House, including a visit from Santa, takes place during the first weekend in Dec.

Admission is free, but the Society welcomes donations. Photography, including use of flash, is permitted. There's ample free parking near the buildings.

Address: 381 E. Main St., P.O. Box 12, Smithville, OH 44677. Phone: 330-263-1481, 669-3231, or 669-2087.

South Euclid:
South Euclid Hist. Soc. Museum

Operated by the South Euclid Historical Society, this museum is located in the caretaker's building of an old estate now housing the South Euclid-Lyndhurst branch of the Cuyahoga County Library. Of special interest to many is a microfilm reader and reels containing images of early area newspapers.

The museum contains items from the late 1800's and early 1900's in what is now South Euclid. Among these items are kitchen utensils, a washing machine, milk bottles, musical instruments, a Victor phonograph, and mementoes from the Bluestone Quarries, an early local source of sandstone.

Other items on display include antique furniture, dolls, toys, and an early Howe treadle sewing machine.

The museum is open every Saturday from 1:00 PM to 4:00 PM. Admission is free. There's free parking on a lot next to the building. Photography, including use of flash, is permitted at the curator's discretion.

Address: 4645 Mayfield Rd., South Euclid, OH 44121. Phone: 216-691-0314 or 440-449-1997.

Strongsville:
Strongsville Historical Village

One of the pioneer settlements of Northeast Ohio, Strongsville was named after an early miller, John Strong. It consists of a collection of pioneer and later buildings in the center of the city. Owned and operated by the local Historical Society, the Village includes eight buildings open for visiting individually or in groups on guided tours. The eight are:

1. Lathrop House. Built in 1871 in Albion, OH, by Hazen Lathrop, son of Thaddeus Lathrop. He in turn was the first miller employed in 1820 at John Strong's mill in Albion, a small settlement just north of the center of what is now Strongsville. The house is built in the Victorian Italianate style.

2. Roe-Chapman Barn. Built on the present site in 1909. Contains a collection of tools and implements from early 1800s to mid-1900s.

3. Log Cabin. Built here in 1976 to show Ohio frontier life from 1816 to 1825. Furnished with pieces from the early 1800s.

4. Roe-Chapman House. A Dutch Colonial Revival house, built in 1904, with a variety of antique furnishings.

5. Bradley House. A small Greek Revival brick house built in Albion in 1832.

6. General Store. Served a crossroads area known as "Beebetown" until 1964. Now offers gift items, candy, pottery, and souvenirs.

7. Academy. Built in 1842; features many artifacts from 10 one-room schoolhouses that dotted the area. Also contains the Roe Millinery, a collection of over 600 wo-

men's hats, hat pins, feathers, wigs, and related items.

8. Baldwin House. An early Western Reserve cottage built by Dr. Baldwin, the area's second physician, in 1823. In the basement you can see an exhibit of HO-gauge trains.

Strongsville Historical Village is open to the public May 1 through Oct. 31, on Wed., Sat., and Sun., from 1:00 PM to 4:00 PM. Special arrangements can be made for guided tours.

Photography, including use of flash, is permitted throughout the village. There is ample free parking at the nearby Strongsville Library and at the Center Middle School.

Admission: $3.00 adults and seniors, $1.00 children 6-18. Children under 6 get in free with an adult. Group rates and annual and life memberships are offered.

Address: 13305 Pearl Rd., Strongsville, OH 44136. Phone: 440-572-0057 or 440-238-6770. The Village is 1/4-mi. north of SR 82 on Pearl Rd.

Sugarcreek:
Alpine Hills Historical Museum

Opened in 1978, this three-story museum in central Sugarcreek recalls the early days of Swiss, German, and Amish settlers in the area. Notable displays include:

* Horse-drawn farm machinery and tools used by area farmers.

* An 1895 firehouse with hand-operated pumper pulled by firemen.

* An 1890 cheese house.

* A letterpress printing shop, where formerly the "Budget" Amish newspaper was printed.

* An 1880 bedroom, completely furnished.

* Costumes from about 1900.

* An 1890-1920 Amish kitchen, complete with wood cook-stove, dry sink, pitcher pump, and other typical furnishings.

* A rifle-making machine shop from the early 1800's.

There are many instructive audio-visual presentations you

can view. A Tourist Information Center in the lobby offers complete details on what to see and do in the Sugarcreek area. A mini-theater shows a 10-min. video presentation on cheesemaking, area industries, and the Amish way of life.

The museum is open Mon.-Sat., Apr. 1-June 30, 10:00 AM to 4:30 PM; July 1-Sept. 30, 9:00 AM to 4:30 PM; and Oct. 1-Nov. 30, 10:00 AM to 4:30 PM. Closed on Sun. Admission is free; donations welcome.

Photography, including use of flash, is permitted. There's free parking on nearby streets.

Address: 106 W. Main St., Sugarcreek, OH 44681. Phone: 330-852-4113.

Twinsburg:
Twinsburg Hist. Soc. Museum

A 1965 schoolhouse is home to this museum, which focuses on the history of Twinsburg and the surrounding area. On display are exhibits of 19th Century furniture, tools, toys, costumes, and miscellaneous artifacts, along with historic photos and engravings. Activities include guided tours, demonstrations, and biannual quilt shows.

The museum is open from the last Sun. of Apr. until Nov. 30, 2:00 PM to 5:00 PM, and at other times by appointment. Admission is free; donations welcome.

Photography is allowed, but no flash. You'll find free parking next to the building and on nearby streets.

Address: 8996 Darrow Rd., P.O. Box 7, Twinsburg, OH 44087. Phone: 330-487-5565.

Vermilion:
Inland Seas Maritime Museum

Paintings, photos, artifacts, newspaper clippings, and model ships tell the story of Great Lakes shipping. The story begins in Aug., 1679, when Robert Cavalier, Sieur de LaSalle sailed his "Griffon" west and north in search of furs, and continues to the present day.

Also on display is the "Canopus" wheelhouse, which gives you a feel for piloting a Great Lakes freighter. See timbers from Admiral Perry's "Niagara," the lens from the Spectacle Reef Lighthouse, and a full-size replica of Vermilion Lighthouse.

The museum is open seven days a week, year around, except on major U.S. holidays. Hours are 10:00 AM to 5:00 PM. Admission: $5.00 adults, $4.00 seniors, $3.00 children 6–18. Younger children get in free. There's a family rate of $10.00, and special rates for groups, by reservation.

Photography is allowed, but no flash for certain exhibits (check with the desk). You can park on the museum lot or nearby streets.

Address: 480 Main St., Vermilion, OH 44089. Phone: 440-867-3467 or 800-893-1485.

Directions: The museum is two miles north of the intersection of SRs 2 and 60, on Main St.

Warren:
John S. Edwards House

Located in the 1807 John S. Edwards residence, this museum collects, preserves, and displays artifacts and books from Warren in the early 1800's. On display are collections of quilts, tools, costumes, musical instruments, furniture, and other antiques. For research, you may access a 100-volume library of historical publications. There's a gift shop on the premises.

Open year around, Sat. and Sun., 1:00 PM to 4:00 PM, and at other times by appointment. Admission is $2.00 adults, $1.00 children 12–18, 50 cents children under 12. Guided tours can be arranged.

Photography, including use of flash, is permitted. You'll find limited free parking on nearby streets.

Address: 303 Monroe St. NW, Warren, OH 44483. Phone: 330-394-4653.

Wellington:
Spirit of '76 Museum

Archibald M. Willard, a Wellington wagon–painter in the late 1800's, created the most famous fine–art painting depicting the American Revolution. Called "The Spirit of '76," it shows two drummers and a fife–player marching ahead of a flag–bearer and a column of soldiers. The original 8–ft. by 10–ft. canvas hangs in Abbott Hall, Marblehead, Mass., but this museum in Wellington, Ohio, displays a large copy and over a dozen original Willard paintings.

Also in the museum, administered by the Southern Lorain County Historical Society, are many artifacts from early days in Lorain County. See especially the spinning wheels, sewing machines, clothing, china, and glassware. Other attractions include antique kitchen and laundry equipment, cheesemaking equipment, and historic photos.

The museum is open Apr. 1–Oct. 31, on Sat. and Sun., 2:30 PM to 5:00 PM. Closed on major U.S. holidays.

Admission is free. No photography allowed. There is free parking on the street.

Address: 201 N. Main St., P.O. Box 76, Wellington, OH 44090. Phone: 440–647–4576.

SECTION 7 -- WESTERVILLE THROUGH ZOAR

Westerville:
Hanby House

Benjamin R. Hanby, who lived here from 1853 to 1870, was a teacher, abolitionist, and minister. In addition, he was a prolific songwriter, and for that he became famous. Hanby wrote about 80 songs, including the Christmas classic "Up on the Housetop" and the pre-Civil War song called "Darling Nelly Gray."

Here, in the only Ohio museum devoted to a composer, you can see a walnut desk he made, his flute, original plates for the first edition of "Darling Nelly Gray," and a large collection of sheet music and books of Hanby songs.

The house is on the National Register of Historic Places, and contains many pieces of furniture belonging to or associated with the Hanby family. The Westerville Historical Society, under an agreement with the Ohio Historical Society, maintains and operates this "house museum."

Hanby House is open May 1-Sept. 30, Sat. 1:00 PM to 4:00 PM, and Sun. 1:00 PM to 4:00 PM. Groups of five or more may tour the museum at other times, by appointment.

Admission: $2.00 adults, $1.60 AAA seniors, $0.75 visitors 6-18. Children under 6 get in free with an adult. For groups of adults numbering 10 or more, the fee is $1.75 each. There is a minimum fee of $10.00 when you schedule by appointment.

Photography, including use of flash, is permitted. There's free parking nearby.

Address: 160 W. Main St., Westerville, OH 43081. Phone: 614-891-6289 or 800-600-6843.

Westerville:
Ross C. Purdy Museum of Ceramics

From 1921 to 1946, Ross Coffin Purdy served as secretary and editor for The American Ceramic Society. His career and extensive collection of ceramic objects comprise the backbone of this museum.

Today, the collection has grown to more than 2,500 pieces. They represent a cross-section of traditional and high-tech ceramics produced since about 1850. The museum displays a large portion of the collection at any given time, with rotating exhibits occasionally showing the balance of the collection.

Sponsorship for the museum comes partly from Saint-Gobain, the French leader in ceramics design, science, and manufacturing.

Included in the exhibits are fine pottery, glasswork, and elaborate ceramic art pieces. Also on display you will find many commercial ceramic products, including bricks, tile, table glassware, and dinnerware.

Among the high-tech pieces on display are space-shuttle nose tiles, a working auto engine with ceramic parts, military armor, and advanced sporting goods with ceramic parts.

Exhibits of "bioceramics" show a ceramic heart valve, a ceramic hip-joint implant, replacement bones for the middle ear, and dental implants.

The museum is open year around, Mon.-Fri., 8:00 AM to 5:00 PM. or by appointment. Closed on Sat., Sun., and major U.S. holidays. Guided tours can be arranged.

Admission is free. Photography, including use of flash, is allowed. There's free parking nearby.

Address: 735 Ceramic Place, Westerville, OH 43081. Phone: 614-890-4700. Fax: 614-899-6109.

Westlake:
Clague House Museum

Robert Clague (b. 1802, d. 1865) immigrated from the Isle of Man and settled in Dover -- now Westlake -- in 1829. A few years later, he returned to the Isle, where he married Margaret Cowell (b. 1810, d. 1884). In 1837 the two moved to Dover, built a log cabin, and began farming. Their nine children took up farming and other occupations.

By about 1850, the Clagues replaced the log cabin with a frame house, and in 1876, with the present brick house. Today it is operated by the Westlake Historical Society as a museum and memorial to Westlake's outstanding pioneer family. The house is listed in the National Register of Historic Places.

On display in the front parlor are original pieces of Clague family furniture, including a family Bible, table, and pump organ. You also can view an original Manx grandfather clock, a Steinway baby grand piano, and a collection of historic clothing. Most pieces in the collection are from the late 1800's and early 1900's. A special feature is a miniature doll-house replica of the museum, completely furnished.

The museum is open 11 months a year, Feb. 1–Dec. 31, on Sundays only, from 2:00 PM to 4:30 PM. Closed in Jan. and on major U.S. holidays. Tours by groups can be arranged.

Admission is free. Photography, including use of flash, is permitted. There's parking next to the building.

Throughout the year, the Society holds special events at the museum. These include an annual antique show in July, demonstrations of pioneer life, and presentations by local historians. Phone or write for details.

Address: 1371 Clague Rd., P.O. Box 45064, Westlake, OH 44145. Phone: 440-835-0778.

Willard:
B&O Railroad Museum

Owned and operated by the Willard Area Historical Society, this museum is located in a depot rebuilt in 1972 from bricks, windows, and other parts from the original 1875 B&O depot. You can view displays of trainman and stewardess uniforms, dining-car china, and other railroad memorabilia.   Outdoors, you can climb up into a 1925 wood-sided caboose and a steel boxcar. These were donated to the museum by the Chessie System, which bought the B&O in 1972.

Inside the boxcar is a 30-ft. N-gauge model of the Willard Railroad Yards, plus other memorabilia.

The museum and rolling stock are open Memorial Day through Labor Day, Sundays only, 1:00 PM to 4:00 PM. Open at other times by appointment.

Admission is free; donations welcome. Photography, including use of flash, is permitted. There's free parking next to the depot.

Address: Main St., SR 103, Willard, OH 44890. Phone: 419-935-0954 or 419-935-0791.

Willowick:
U.S. Aviation Museum

Located in the Shoregate Shopping Center behind K-B Toys, this museum displays scale models of U.S. Navy and U.S. Army Air Force combat aircraft from World War II. Almost all the models are made at the 1/48 scale, to give you correct comparisons. Some models have wingspans of more than two ft.

A few of the famous aircraft on display in model form are the B-17 Flying Fortress, B-29 Super Fortress, P-51 Mustang, P-47 Thunderbolt, F4U Corsair, P-38 Lightning, and F7F Tigercat.

Also on display are World War II aviation artifacts and memorabilia, such as instruments, uniforms, and unit shoulder patches. The building contains an aviation library and gift shop. In the latter, you will find genuine military-issue dogtags, shirts, hats, posters, and airplane models.

Exhibits include restorations of a World War II Link Trainer, aircraft flight panels, and surface controls.

The museum holds free public meetings at 7:30 PM on the last Thursday of every month. Usually there is a guest speaker. Feel free to call the museum for news about talks and special activities.

Hours: Open year around on Tues. and Fri. 10:00 AM to 6:00 PM, and Sat. 12:00 noon to 5:00 PM. Admission is free. Group tours can be arranged.

Photography, including use of flash, is permitted. There is

ample free parking nearby.

Address: 29690 Lakeshore Blvd., Willowick, OH 44095. Phone: 440-516-8726. E-mail: USAM1 @ Juno.com.

Wooster:
College of Wooster Art Museum

In some 2,500 sq. ft. of floor space in two galleries, this museum holds four to six fine-arts exhibitions each year. A recent traveling exhibit was entitled "Hung Liu: A Ten-Year Survey, 1988-1998." Permanent collections include African art, ancient and contemporary ceramics, and Chinese art.

Visitors can participate in gallery walks plus periodic lectures and exhibit openings. Admission is free. No photography allowed.

The museum is open Sept. 1-May 31, Mon.-Fri., 10:30 AM to 4:30 PM, and on Sun., 1:00 PM to 5:00 PM. Closed on Sat. and major U.S. holidays.

Address: Ebert Art Center, 1220 Beall Ave., Wooster, OH 44691. Phone: 330-263-2495. Fax: 330-263-2633.

Directions: Located on Beall Ave. between Wayne Ave. and University Ave. There is free parking on nearby lots.

Wooster:
Wayne County Hist. Soc. Campus

From the early 1800's on, Wayne County was settled in large part by New England Yankees and German-Americans from Pennsylvania. Their heritage endures in a cluster of structures owned and preserved in Wooster by the Wayne County Historical Society. The "campus" includes:

* The Reasin Beall Homestead. A large brick house built in 1815-17 by a noted Revolutionary War general, this structure is being furnished and decorated to look the way it did in the early 1800's.

* Ladies' Dress Shop. Holds a collection of women's fashions from the early 1800's on.

* 1873 Schoolhouse. A one-room building moved here

159

from Wooster's southern edge. With its potbellied stove, McGuffey Readers, and other artifacts, it recalls an old-fashioned place of learning.

* Log Cabin. An original from the early 1800's, this house was moved to the campus from the original site in 1963. Authentically furnished.

* Outdoor Bake Oven. Moved here from a farm near Kidron, this large oven is typical of the ovens found in early German farms during the 1800's.

* Kister Building. The Society's main museum, this structure contains rotating exhibits, a library, and a carriage barn. Among the attractions is a "stuffed squirrel band."

The campus is open for touring year around on Tues.-Sun., 2:00 PM to 4:30 PM. Closed on Mon. and major U.S. holidays. Special tours can be arranged.

Admission: $3.00 adults and seniors, free to students and children under 6. Special rates for large groups.

No photography permitted. There is free parking nearby.

Address: 546 E. Bowman St., Wooster, OH 44691. Phone: 330-362-8856.

Worthington:
Worthington Museums

The Worthington Historical Society has preserved and re-stored two historic structures and converted them into museums. One is the Orange Johnson House Museum at 956 High St. Built in 1811, it was opened for touring in 1972. This is the only pioneer home in Franklin County on its original foundation that is open to the public.

Designed in the Early Federal style, the Orange Johnson House contains furniture, decorations, and artifacts from the early 1800's. Hours are on Sun., 2:00 PM to 5:00 PM, year around except between Christmas and early Feb. Also closed on Easter Sunday.

Admission for non-members is $2.00 adults and seniors, $1.00 youths and children. Members of the WHS get in free.

160

The second museum, The Old Rectory, was built ca. 1845 for St. John's Episcopal Church, the first church of its denomination west of the Alleghenies. Designed in the Greek Revival style, this building houses a doll museum containing dolls and toys from the 1800's. The collection includes German china dolls, Parisian bisques, French fashions, Milliner's models, French "bebes," and many American dolls by famous makers.

The Old Rectory is at 50 W. New England Ave. Admission is by appointment only, and costs $1.50 a person for non-members. Members get in free.

No photography is allowed in either museum. Both have free parking on their grounds and on nearby streets.

To obtain more information, write to: Worthington Historical Society, 50 W. New England Ave., Worthington, OH 43085. Phone: 614-885-1247.

Youngstown:
Arms Family Museum of Local History

Owned and operated by the Mahoning Valley Historical Society, this four-story structure was built in the early 1900's as a showcase of arts and crafts. Wilford and Olive Arms wanted their home to reflect their love of handicrafts, medieval design, and nature.

Today, preserved as a museum, the home has exhibits that explain the history of the Mahoning River Valley. Represented are Indian tribes, pioneer settlers, Welsh coal miners, African American freemen, Eastern European mill workers, and others. Also contained in the building are most of the original Arms Family furniture and decorations, and an archival library.

The museum is open year around on Tues.-Fri., 1:00 PM to 4:00 PM, and on Sat. and Sun., 1:30 PM to 5:00 PM. Closed on Mon. and major U.S. holidays.

Admission: $3.00 adults, $2.00 seniors and college students, and $1.00 visitors under 18. You can schedule group tours with advance notice.

Photography without flash is allowed in some areas; check with your tour guide. There's free parking on the premises.

Address: 648 Wick Ave., Youngstown, OH 44502. Phone: 330-743-2589. Fax: 330-743-7210.

Youngstown:
Butler Institute of American Art

Said to contain one of the most outstanding collections of American (U.S.) art in the country, this museum has works from Colonial times to the present. Among the 5,000-plus pieces are paintings by Copley, Earl, Eakins, Gottlieb, Homer, Heade, Henri, Koch, Leslie, Mitchell, Nevelson, and others.

The museum is famous for its collections of Western, marine, and watercolor paintings. Along with the paintings, Butler has many pieces of ceramic, sculptured, and photographic art. The building contains a library of art books, available for research.

Activities here include guided tours, lectures, film showings, concerts, and temporary and touring exhibits.

The museum is open year around, Tues., Thurs., Fri., and Sat., 11:00 AM to 4:00 PM; also Wed., 11:00 AM to 8:00 PM, and Sun., 12:00 noon to 4:00 PM. Closed on Mon. and major U.S. holidays.

Admission is free; donations welcome. No photography permitted. There is free parking nearby.

Address: 524 Wick Ave., Youngstown, OH 44502. Phone: 330-743-1711. Fax: 330-743-9567.

Youngstown:
Youngstown Historical Center
Of Industry & Labor

The Mahoning Valley's rich deposits of raw materials made it ideal for steelmaking, and by 1920, the Valley was second only to Pittsburgh in steel production in the U.S. But by

1980, the prevalence of steelmaking in the area's economy had faded dramatically.

This museum chronicles the rise and fall of the iron and steel industries in the Youngstown area. A permanent exhibit combines artifacts, videotaped interviews with steel-mill workers and executives, and full-scale recreations of places where steelworkers lived and labored.

The museum is open year around, Wed.-Sat., 9:00 AM to 5:00 PM; and Sun. and some holidays, 12:00 noon to 5:00 PM. Closed every Mon. and on Thanksgiving, Christmas, and New Year's Day.

Admission: $5.00 adults; $4.50 seniors, youths 12-18, and AAA members; and $1.25 children 6-12. Those under 6 get in free with an adult.

Photography, including use of flash, is permitted. There's free parking on the museum grounds.

Address: 151 W. Wood St., Youngstown, OH 44501.
Phone: 330-743-5934 or 800-262-6137.

Zanesville:
Historic District of Zanesville

The Pioneer & Historical Society of Muskingum County, Ohio, manages two historic homes in the Putnam District of Zanesville. The two are called The Stone Academy and the Dr. Increase Mathews House.

Built in 1809, The Stone Academy was constructed by leaders of Putnam (later incorporated into Zanesville) as a possible statehouse for the Ohio legislature. Subsequently the building was used as a boys' school, girls' school, state headquarters for abolitionists, host to conventions, and possible safehouse for runaway slaves. The building then became a private residence, and was the childhood home of Elizabeth Robins, an actress, playwright, and author.

Today, the building serves as an area museum. Displays include revolving exhibits that show historical photos, artifacts, clothing, etc.

The Dr. Increase Mathews House is a three-story residence built of local sandstone by Putnam's founder. The oldest home in Zanesville, it has passed through several families and many alterations.

Now the rooms are furnished and decorated in the modes of several historic periods. In addition, there are permanent exhibits of area military history, river life, and the local pottery industry.

The Stone Academy is open year around, Tues.-Sat., 12:00 noon to 4:00 PM. The Dr. Increase Mathews House has the same hours, but only from Memorial Day to Labor Day. Tours of this house may be scheduled for Sept.-May by appointment. Both buildings are closed on Sun., Mon., and major U.S. holidays.

Admission: $3.00 a person for both buildings, $2.00 for one museum only. Children under 6 get in free with an adult.

Photography, including use of flash, is permitted. There's free street parking for the Doctor's House, and free parking on a lot next to The Stone Academy.

Address: 115 Jefferson St., Zanesville, OH 43701. Phone: 740-454-9500.

Zoar:
Zoar Village State Memorial

In 1817, a group of German separatists -- they had split from the Lutheran Church over theological and political differences -- left southeastern Germany for the new United States. Under their spiritual and temporal leader Joseph Bimeler, they spent 92 days on the Atlantic, arriving in Philadelphia in Aug., 1817.

About half decided to winter there with their Quaker friends and benefactors. The other half set out across Pennsylvania, heading for a 5,500-acre tract they had purchased on the Tuscarawas River southeast of Canton. The first band arrived on Oct. 16, 1817, naming their new settlement "Zoar." This was done in honor of a town in Judea to which Lot and his family fled after the destruction of Sodom. The half that had remained in Philadelphia made the trip to Ohio in 1818.

At first the settlers tried working individually owned plots, but after 18 months they turned to practicing an early, Christian form of communal living in which they shared property and labor. They called themselves "The Society of Separatists of Zoar," and set to work building a community. Virtually all of that village still stands today, a testament to Zoarite skill, patience, and foresight. Today the Ohio Historical Society owns and operates many of the buildings, and oversees any needed restoration.

For a fee, you can tour about 10 historic buildings in Zoar. Among them is Number One House, which displays original furniture, tinware, quilts, and other products made by Zoar craftsmen. Along with the museum, you can tour a bakery, tinshop, wagon shop, smithy, and dairy, plus a communal kitchen, laundry, and storeroom.

Many of Zoar's other original buildings are still in use by private citizens as bed & breakfast lodgings, residences, stores, and a church. You can visit many of these, or simply view them from the outside. Examples are the Zoar Tavern & Inn, Historic Zoar Church, Zoar Schoolhouse, and Adamson's Antique Shop.

Admission tickets, tour arrangements, maps, and literature are available at the Zoar Store, near the south end of Main Street. Admission fees: $5.00 adults, $4.50 seniors, $1.25 children 6–12. Those under 6 get in free with an adult. Group tours at reduced rates are offered.

Zoar Village historical tours are conducted from April through October. Days and times vary according to season; call for details.

Annual special events are a "Harvest Festival" in early Aug., "Apfelfest" in early Oct., and "Christmas in Zoar" in early Dec.

Photography, including use of flash, is allowed in the historic buildings and in the grounds and village gardens. There is free parking in a lot at the south end of the village, and on side streets.

For more information, free literature, and reservations, write to: Zoar Village State Memorial, P.O. Box 404, Zoar, OH 44697. Phone: 330-874-4336 or 800-874-4336.

Directions: From I-77 12 miles south of Canton, get off at Exit 93, the one for Zoar and Bolivar. Go three miles east on SR 212. This road runs south into Zoar as Main St.

Appendices

APPENDIX A -- ADDITIONAL LISTINGS

Museums in this appendix do not have full writeups like those in the main sections because the facilities here are quite small, or are not true museums (but deserve to be listed anyway), or their managements did not provide any information or adequate information even after our attempts to contact them by mail. In one case, the museum did not answer phone calls made during museum hours on six different days.

As in the main sections preceding, museums here are listed alphabetically by city or town, and by museum name. If no phone number is given, it's because none is listed in the local directory, as verified with the area's Information Operator.

Akron: Goodyear World of Rubber, 1144 E. Market St., Akron, OH 44308. History and technology of rubber; includes Charles Goodyear's log cabin. Free admission. Open Mon.-Fri., 8:00 AM to 4:30 PM. Gift shop. Phone: 330-796-7117

Brecksville: Squire Rich Home and Museum, Brecksville Historical Ass'n., SR 21, Brecksville, OH 44141. History

Cambridge: Hopalong Cassidy Museum, 127 S. 10th St., Cambridge, OH 43725. Phone: 740-432-3364. Honors William L. Boyd, who played Hopalong Cassidy in films of 1930's and later. Shows collection of "Hopalong Cassidy endorsed products."

Cambridge: National Cambridge Collectors, P.O. Box 416, Cambridge, OH 43725. Phone: 740-432-4245. Glassware

Canal Winchester: Barber Museum, 2 S. High St., Canal Winchester, OH. Phone: 614-833-9931. Barbering memorabilia

Chillicothe: James M. Thomas Museum, 68 E. Main St., Chillicothe, OH 45601. Phone: 740-772-8200. History

Cleveland: Log Cabin Museum, Cleveland Heritage Park, Merwin & Center Sts., Cleveland, OH 44114. In the Flats. Commemorates spot at which Moses Cleaveland (sic) and his party first landed on the bank of the Cuyahoga River to found the city. Phone: 440-943-5377. Open in June, July, and Aug. on Wed., Fri., and Sat. 11:00 AM to 4:00 PM, and Sun. 1:00 PM to 5:00 PM. History

Cleveland: Rainbow Children's Museum, 10730 Euclid Ave., Cleveland, OH 44106. Phone: 216-791-7114. Children's interests

Columbus: Harley-Davidson Museum, A.D. Farrow Co., 491 W. Broad St., Columbus, OH 43215. Phone: 614-228-6353. Museum of America's oldest Harley dealer. History, motorcycles.

Columbus: Motorcycle Heritage Museum, 33 Collegeview Rd., Columbus, OH 43081. Phone: 614-882-2782. Displays of vintage motorcycles and their histories. In July, 2000, this museum moves to new location at 13515 Yarmouth Rd., Pickerington, OH 43147. Motorcycles

Columbus: Jack Nicklaus Museum, 5750 Memorial Dr., Columbus, OH 43017. Phone: 614-792-2353. Opens in Spring, 2000. Sports

Creston: Creston Hist. Soc. Museum, P.O. Box 2222, Creston, OH 44217. Phone: 330-435-6796. History

Dalton: Dalton Historical Sites, 115 E. Main St., P.O. Box 273, Dalton, OH 44618. Phone: 330-828-2552. History

Fredericktown: Fredericktown Historical Museum, 110 W. Sandusky St., Fredericktown, OH. Phone: 740-694-3805. Artifacts from the 1800's, including clothing, many historical photos. By appointment only.

Gates Mills: Gates Mills Hist. Soc. Museum, 7580 Old Mill Rd., Gates Mills, OH 44040. Phone: 440-423-4808. History

Geneva-on-the-Lake: Ashtabula County History Museum, Route 534, Geneva-on-the-Lake, OH 44041. Phone: 330-466-7337. Open June, July, Aug., on Wed.-Sun. 1:00 PM to 5:00 PM. Mail to: P.O. Box 36, Jefferson, OH 44047. History

Jefferson: J.R. Giddings Law Office Museum, 104 N. Chestnut St., Jefferson, OH 44047. Phone: 330-466-7337. Open year around, Sun. only, 1:00 PM to 4:00 PM or by appointment. Mail to: P.O. Box 36, Jefferson, OH 44047. History, occupation

Kent: Kent State Hearing Aid Museum, Rm. 101, Hearing & Speech Bldg., Kent State University, Kent, OH 44242. Phone: 330-672-2672. Thousands of items spanning the history of hearing aids, including vacuum-tube devices carried by hand, to latest appliances smaller than a dime. Open year around, Mon.-Fri., 8:00 AM to 5:00 PM. Closed Sat. and Sun. Ample parking on university lots. Admission free; guided tours by appointment. Health & medical

Kenton: Dougherty House, 215 N. Detroit St., Kenton, OH 43326. Phone: 419-673-7147. Built in 1875, this historic home one of the pair of buildings listed below. Furnishings commemorate Victorian domestic life. Closed on major U.S. holidays. History

Kenton: Hardin County Historical Museums, 223 N. Main St., Kenton, OH 43326. Two historic buildings in complex. See collection of cast-iron toys. History

Killbuck: Killbuck Valley Museum, Front St., Killbuck, OH 44637. History

Kirtland: Euclid Beach Amusement Park Museum, 9193 Chillicothe Rd., SR 306, Kirtland, OH 44094. Memorabilia

Lenox: Lenox Rural Museum, 2510 SR 46, Lenox, OH 44047. Phone: 330-224-2640. Open June, July, and Aug., Sun. only, 2:00 PM to 4:00 PM or by appointment. Mail to: P.O. Box 56, Jefferson, OH 44047. Location: On SR 46 in Ashtabula County, about 4 miles south of Jefferson. History, rural

Lisbon: Fort Tuscaroras Museum, Lisbon, OH 44432. Phone: 330-855-3041. History

Loudonville: Mohican Hist. Soc. Museum. See listing for the Cleo Redd Fisher Museum, Loudonville. History

Mansfield: Living Bible Museum, 500 Tingley Ave., Mansfield, OH 44905. Phone: 419-524-0139. Bible

Marshallville: Marshallville Hist. Soc. Museum, 4 E. Church St., Marshallville, OH 44645. Phone:330-855-3041. History

Massillon: Military History Museum, Ohio Society of Military History, 319 Lincoln Way East, Massillon, OH 44646. Phone: 330-832-5553. Military

Milan: Edna Roe Newton Memorial Bldg., 10 Edison Dr., Milan, OH 44846. Phone: 419-499-2968. Part of the Milan Historical Museum, a seven-building complex. History, fine-arts collections

Millersburg: Yoder's Amish Home, 6050 SR 515, Millersburg, OH 44654. Phone: 330-893-2541. Tour two Amish homes on a 116-acre working farm. Has animal petting area, buggy rides, horse-drawn hay rides, craft demonstrations. Store sells handmade items such as quilts, chairs, dolls. Open mid-Apr. to Oct. 31., Mon.-Sat., 10:00 AM to 5:00 PM. Open on Memorial Day, July Fourth, and Labor Day. Ethnic, religious interests.

New London: New London Historical Museum, 150 Coleman St., New London, OH 44851. History

Northfield: Palmer House Museum, 9390 Old Eight Rd., P.O. Box 99, Northfield, OH 44067. Phone: 216-237-1813. History

Orrville: Orrville Historical Museum, 142 Depot St., P.O. Box 137, Orrville, OH 44667. History

Plymouth: Plymouth Area Museum, 15 Sandusky St., Plymouth, OH 44870. Phone: 419-687-1435. History

Rittman: Pioneer House Museum, Rittman Hist. Soc., P.O. Box 583, Rittman, OH 44270. Phone: 330-927-7572. History

Salem: Burchfield Homestead, 837 E. Fourth St., Salem, OH 44460. Phone: 330-332-8601. Home for many years of Charles Burchfield, noted Ohio artist. Contains over 70 reproductions of his more famous works. Art & furnishings

Shreve: County Line Museum, County Line Hist. Soc. of Wayne and Holmes Counties, P.O. Box 614, Shreve, OH 44676. Phone: 330-378-2121. History

Shreve: Kister Water Mill, 3936 Kister Rd., Shreve, OH 44676. Phone: 330-567-3500. History

Steubenville: Jefferson County Hist. Ass'n., 426 Franklin Ave., P.O. Box 4268, Steubenville, OH 43952. History

Warren: National Packard Museum, 1899 Mahoning Ave. NW, Warren, OH. Phone: 330-394-8484. Antique Packard automobiles

Willoughby: History Center of Willoughby, Little Red Schoolhouse Society, Inc., 5040 Shankland Rd., Willoughby, OH 44094. Phone: 440-975-3740. History

Windsor: Christ Episcopal Church Museum, Route 322 & Wiswell Rd., Windsor, OH 44099. Phone: 330–272–5174 or 330–272–5102. Open Memorial Day through Labor Day, Sun. only, 1:00 PM to 4:00 PM or by appointment. Religious; church museum

Youngstown: McDonough Museum of Art, Youngstown State University, One University Plaza, Youngstown, OH 44555. Phone: 330–742–3627. Fine arts

Zanesville: Zanesville Art Center, 620 Military Road, Zanesville, OH 43701. Phone: 740–452–0741. Fine arts

APPENDIX B -- INDEX BY SUBJECT

Following are names and locations of museums that spe-
cialize in certain subjects, or that have significant collections pertaining to certain subjects. These museums are listed
in alphabetical order by name of subject.

The majority of museums, villages, and historic districts
described in this guidebook concern the history of the locale,
meaning the town or city and its surrounding countryside. A
few such as the Firelands Museum and Western Reserve
History Museum cover a region, while the Ohio Historical
Center gives information pertaining to the entire state. For
information about a given town or city, see the Table of
Contents.

It is important to note that most museums contain a broad
range of items. For instance, any given history museum may
display specimens of historic toys, dolls, furniture, handicrafts (e.g., quilts), china, glassware, clothing, utensils,
firearms, and so on. Some historical museums even contain
specimens of fine art; for instance, see Stan Hywet Hall in
Akron. If you have an interest in a particular subject listed,
therefore, it would be useful to scan the entire guidebook.

Air & Space
Int'l. Women's Air & Space Museum, Cleveland, p. 58
MAPS Air Museum, North Canton, p. 128
NASA John Glenn Visitor Center, Cleveland, p. 60
Ohio History of Flight Museum, Columbus, p. 73
U.S. Aviation Museum, Willowick, p. 158

Applicances
Hoover Historical Center, North Canton, p. 127
Victorian Perambulator Museum, Jefferson, p. 98

Arts & Furnishings
(This category includes the fine arts -- paintings, sculpture,
pottery, glass, etc. -- plus furniture, wall coverings, tapestries, and some religious art. Also see listings of history
museums.)
Akron Art Museum, Akron, p. 21

Autos & Aviation

Canals; Ohio & Erie Canal, Milan Canal

Ceramics
(Also see Arts & Furnishings preceeding.)

Children's Interests

Clothing, Fashions, Costumes, Uniforms
(Also see historical museums in Contents.)

Crafts
(Also see historical museums in Contents.)
MAPS Air Museum, North Canton, p. 128
Ohio Craft Museum, Columbus, p. 72
Warther's Carvings Museum, Dover, p. 83

Ethnic
Cleveland Hungarian Heritage Museum, Euclid, p. 88
Croatian Heritage Museum, Eastlake, p. 86
Romanian Ethnic Art Museum, Cleveland, p. 61
Schrock's Amish Farm & Home, Berlin, p. 35
Ukranian Museum and Archives, Cleveland, p. 63
Yoder's Amish Home, Millersburg, p. 170

Glass
(This category includes art glass and fine manufactured
pieces. Also see the Ceramics and Arts & Furnishings
categories preceeding.)
Cambridge Glass Museum, Cambridge, p. 38
Degenhart Paperweight & Glass Museum, Cambridge, p. 39
National Cambridge Collectors, Cambridge, p. 167
National Heisey Glass Museum, Newark, p. 124

Health & Medicine
Dittrick Museum of Medical History, Cleveland, p. 54
Health Museum of Cleveland, Cleveland, p. 57
Kent State Hearing Aid Museum, Kent, p. 169

History
(Most of the museums, historic villages, etc., listed in this
book pertain to local or regional history. For historical information about a particular town, look for it in the Table
of Contents, or look for a city nearby.)

Indians (Native Americans)
(Many small, local museums display Indian artifacts found
nearby.)
Cleveland Museum of Natural History, Cleveland, p. 50
Indian Museum of Lake County, Painesville, p. 138

Literary
Malabar Farm, Lucas, p. 106
Thurber House, Columbus, p. 76

Marine, Great Lakes, Maritime, Navy
Ashtabula Marine Museum, Ashtabula, p. 26
Columbus Santa Maria, Columbus, p. 69
Fairport Marine Museum, Fairport Harbor, p. 90
Inland Seas Maritime Museum, Vermilion, p. 152
Lake Erie Islands Museum, Put-in-Bay, p. 140
Perry Memorial Museum, Put-in-Bay, p. 140
Sandusky Area Maritime Museum, Sandusky, p. 145
Steamship W.G. Mather Museum, Cleveland, p. 62
U.S.S. Cod Submarine Museum, Cleveland, p. 64

Military, Wars
Cleveland Museum of Art, Cleveland, p. 49
Follett House Museum, Sandusky, p. 143
Fort Laurens State Memorial, Bolivar, p. 36
Fort Tuscaroras, Lisbon, p. 170
Lake Erie Islands Museum, Put-in-Bay, p. 140
McCook Civil War Museum, Carrollton, p. 47
Military History Museum, Massillon, p. 170
103rd Ohio Infantry Museum, Sheffield Lake, p. 147
Perry Memorial Museum, Put-in-Bay, p. 140
U.S.S. Cod Submarine Museum, Cleveland, p. 64

Motorcycles
Harley-Davidson Museum, Columbus, p. 168
Massillon Museum, Massillon, p. 110
Motorcycle Heritage Museum, Columbus, p. 168

Music
Dan Emmett House, Mount Vernon, p. 122
Hanby House, Westerville, p. 155
National Polka Hall of Fame, Euclid, p. 89
Rock & Roll Hall of Fame and Museum, Cleveland, p. 61

Nature, Natural History
Cleveland Museum of Natural History, Cleveland, p. 50
Lake Erie Nature and Science Center, Bay Village, p. 30
Orton Geological Museum, Columbus, p. 75

Police, Prisons
Akron Police Dept. Museum, Akron, p. 21
Cleveland Police Hist. Soc. Museum, Cleveland, p. 51
Ohio State Reformatory, Mansfield, p. 108

Railroads, Trolleys
B&O Railroad Museum, Willard, p. 157
Conneaut Historical Railroad Museum, Conneaut, p. 77
Dennison Railroad Depot Museum, Dennison, p. 81
Jefferson Depot Railroad Museum, Jefferson, p. 97
Middlefield Railroad Depot Museum, Middlefield, p. 116
Orrville Railroad Depot Museum, Orrville, p. 135
Trolleyville USA, Olmsted Twp., p. 135

Religious
Kirtland Temple Historic Center, Kirtland, p. 100
Living Bible Museum, Mansfield, p. 170
Romanian Ethnic Art Museum, Cleveland, p. 61
Yoder's Amish Home, Millersburg, p. 170

Science & Industry
Auman Museum of Radio & Television, Dover, p. 81
Center of Science and Industry (COSI), Columbus, p. 67
Edison's Birthplace Museum, Milan, p. 117
Goodyear World of Rubber, Akron, p. 167
Great Lakes Science Center, Cleveland, p. 56
Inventure Place, Akron, p. 23

Sports
Pro Football Hall of Fame and Museum, Canton, p. 46

Toys, Dolls, Amusements
(A number of historical museums have doll collections, plus examples of antique toys.)

Trades, Occupations

APPENDIX C -- INDEX BY NAME OF MUSEUM

103rd Ohio Infantry Museum, Sheffield Lake, p. 147

A

African American Museum, Cleveland, p. 48
Akron Art Museum, Akron, p. 21
Akron Police Dept. Museum, Akron, p. 21
Allen Memorial Art Museum, Oberlin, p. 133
Alpine Hills Historical Museum, Sugarcreek, p. 151
Arms Family Museum, Youngstown, p. 161
Ashland County Historical Museum, Ashland, p. 25
Ashtabula Cty. Hist. Museum, Geneva-on-the-Lake, p. 169
Ashtabula Marine Museum, Ashtabula, p. 26
Auman Museum of Radio & Television, Dover, p. 81
Aurora Museum, Aurora, p. 27

B

Barber Museum, Canal Winchester, p. 167
Batavia Inn, Middlefield, p. 116
B&O Railroad Museum, Willard, p. 157
Bedford Hist. Soc. Museum, Bedford, p. 31
Bexley Hist. Soc. Museum, Bexley, p. 35
Brooklyn Hist. Soc. Museum, Brooklyn, p. 37
Burchfield Homestead, Salem, p. 171
Butler Institute of American Art, Youngstown, p. 162

C

Cambridge Glass Museum, Cambridge, p. 38
Canal Fulton Heritage Soc. Museums, Canal Fulton, p. 41
Canton Classic Car Museum, Canton, p. 43
Canton Museum of Art, Canton, p. 44
Center of Science and Industry (COSI), Columbus, p. 67
Century Village, Burton, p. 37
Christ Episcopal Church Museum, Windsor, p. 172
Clague House Museum, Westlake, p. 156
Cleo Redd Fisher Museum, Loudonville, p. 105

179

D

E

F

Fisher (C.R.) Museum, Loudonville, p. 105
Five Oaks Historic Home, Massillon, p. 110
Follett House Museum, Sandusky, p. 143
Fort Laurens State Memorial, Bolivar, p. 36
Fort Tuscaroras Museum, Lisbon, p. 170
Fredericktown Historical Museum, Fredericktown, p. 168
Frostville Museum, North Olmsted, p. 130

G

Garfield Birthsite, Moreland Hills, p. 119
Garfield Heights Historical Museum, p. 91
Garfield National Historic Site, Mentor, p. 113
Gates Mills Hist. Soc. Museum, Gates Mills, p. 169
Gay 90's Mansion Museum, Barnesville, p. 27
Giddings (J.R.) Law Office Museum, Jefferson, p. 169
Gnadenhutten Historical Park, Gnadenhutten, p. 92
Goodyear World of Rubber, Akron, p. 167
Granville Historical Museum, Granville, p. 94
Granville Lifestyle Museum, Granville, p. 94
Great Lakes Science Center, Cleveland, p. 56
Guernsey County Museum, Cambridge, p. 39

H

Hale Farm and Village, Bath, p. 28
Hanby House, Westerville, p. 155
Hardin County Historical Museums, Kenton, p. 169
Harley-Davidson Museum, Columbus, p. 168
Health Museum of Cleveland, Cleveland, p. 57
Heritage Hall Museum, Lakeside, p. 101
Heritage Museum of Kappa Kappa Gamma, Columbus, p. 70
Hickories Museum, Elyria, p. 87
Historic District of Zanesville, Zanesville, p. 163
Historic Lyme Village, Bellevue, p. 32
History Center of Willoughby, Willoughby, p. 171
Hoover Historical Center, North Canton, p. 127
Hopalong Cassidy Museum, Cambridge, p. 167

I

Indian Museum of Lake County, Painesville, p. 138
Inland Seas Maritime Museum, Vermilion, p. 152
Int'l. Women's Air & Space Museum, Cleveland, p. 58
Inventure Place, Akron, p. 23

J

Jack Nicklaus Museum -- see Nicklaus (Jack) Museum
James M. Thomas Museum, Chillicothe, p. 168
J.E. Reeves Home and Museum, Dover, p. 82
J.R. Giddings Law Office Museum, Jefferson, p. 169
J.S. Edwards House, Warren, p. 153
Jefferson County Hist. Ass'n., Steubenville, p. 171
Jefferson Depot Railroad Museum, Jefferson, p. 97
John Johnson Farm House, Hiram, p. 96
John Smart House, Medina, p. 112

K

Kelton House Museum and Garden, Columbus, p. 71
Kent State Hearing Aid Museum, Kent, p. 169
Kent State Univ. Museum, Kent, p. 99
Kidron Community Hist. Soc. Museum, Kidron, p. 99
Killbuck Valley Museum, Killbuck, p. 169
Kingwood Center, Mansfield, p. 107
Kirtland Temple Historic Center, Kirtland, p. 100
Kister Water Mill, Shreve, p. 171
Knox County Agricultural Museum, Mount Vernon, p. 122
Knox County Hist. Soc. Museum, Mount Vernon, p. 123

L

Lake County History Center, Mentor, p. 114
Lake Erie Islands Museum, Put-in-Bay, p. 140
Lake Erie Nature and Science Center, Bay Village, p. 30
Lake View Cemetery, Cleveland, p. 59
Lenox Rural Museum, Lenox, p. 170
Lisbon Historic District, Lisbon, p. 103
Little Red Schoolhouse Museum, Maple Heights, p. 109
Living Bible Museum, Mansfield, p. 170
Log Cabin Museum, Cleveland, p. 168

Log House Museum, Columbiana, p. 67
Loghurst Farm Museum, Canfield, p. 42
Lyme Village (Historic), Bellevue, p. 32

M

Mahler Museum, Berea, p. 33
Malabar Farm, Lucas, p. 106
MAPS Air Museum, North Canton, p. 128
Marshallville Hist. Soc. Museum, Marshallville, p. 170
Massillon Museum, Massillon, p. 110
Mayfield Twp. Hist. Soc. Museum, Mayfield, p. 112
McCook Civil War Museum, Carrollton, p. 47
McDonough Museum of Art, Youngstown, p. 172
McKinley Birthplace Memorial, Niles, p. 127
McKinley (The) Museum, Canton, p. 45
Merry-Go-Round Museum, Sandusky, p. 144
Middlefield Railroad Depot Museum, Middlefield, p. 116
Mid-Ohio Historical Museum, Canal Winchester, p. 41
Milan Historical Museum, Milan, p. 118
Military History Museum, Massillon, p. 170
Mohican Hist. Soc. Museum, Loudonville -- see
   Cleo Redd Fisher Museum, Loudonville, p. 105
Monroe (James) House, Oberlin, p. 133
Moore House Museum, Lorain, p. 104
Motorcycle Heritage Museum, Columbus, p. 168
Mount Pleasant Historical Center, Mount Pleasant, p. 120
Museum of Ceramics, East Liverpool, p. 85

N

NASA John Glenn Visitor Center, Cleveland, p. 60
National Cambridge Collectors, Cambridge, p. 167
National First Ladies' Library, Canton, p. 46
National Heisey Glass Museum, Newark, p. 124
National Polka Hall of Fame, Euclid, p. 89
National Packard Museum, Warren, p. 171
National Road/Zane Gray Museum, Norwich, p. 132
New London Historical Museum, New London, p. 171
Newton (Edna Roe) Memorial Building, Milan, p. 170
Nicklaus (Jack) Museum, Columbus, p. 168
N.K. Whitney Store Museum, Kirtland, p. 101

O

P

R

S

T

U

V

W

Y

Z

APPENDIX D -- ABOUT THE AUTHOR

Joseph C. Quinlan is a retired trade-magazine editor, now working part-time as a freelance magazine writer, book writer, and publisher. As of this writing, he has had over 490 articles published. He sold some 60 of them as a freelancer, along with dozens of original photos.

After receiving his B.S. degree in Journalism from Marquette University, Milwaukee, Wis., he served on active duty in the U.S. Army Artillery for three years. He then worked as a publicist for three manufacturers, a PR agency writer and account executive, and magazine editor. His last post before retirement was that of editor-in-chief of *Quality in Manufacturing* Magazine.

Quinlan won the 1981 American Business Press (ABP) Jesse H. Neal Award for a series of articles in *Material Handling Engineering* Magazine. He is author of the book "Industrial Publicity," published in 1983 by Van Nostrand Reinhold, New York.

Quinlan and his wife Marjorie have personally visited many of the facilities listed in this book. Others were surveyed by mail and phone.

He is a member of the National Trust for Historic Preservation and the Cleveland Museum of Art.

Order Page

To order more copies of this book:

Each copy costs $14.95 plus $0.75 Ohio sales tax and $2.50 for shipping and handling, or a total of $18.20 a copy. To order a copy, write to: Global Editorial Co. Dept. OP, P.O. Box 210058, Cleveland, OH 44121.

Payment is by check or money order only. Sorry, no phone or credit-card orders.

If you are purchasing books for a museum or library, and you want three or more copies, write for a special order form. You are entitled to a special discount.

Satisfaction guaranteed. Thank you for your interest.